RUNNING TOWARD
STILLNESS

RUNNING TOWARD STILLNESS

STEPHEN LEGAULT

RMB

Rocky Mountain Books
www.rmbooks.com

Library and Archives Canada Cataloguing in Publication

Legault, Stephen, 1971–, author
Running toward stillness / Stephen Legault.

Issued in print and electronic formats.
ISBN 978-1-927330-64-7 (pbk.).— ISBN 978-1-927330-65-4 (html).—
ISBN 978-1-927330-66-1 (pdf)

1. Nature—Psychological aspects. 2. Running—Psychological aspects.
3. Meditation. 4. Mental health. 5. Landscapes—Pictorial works. I. Title.

BF353.5.N37L44 2013   155.9'1   C2013-903113-8
C2013-903114-6

Front cover photo: *barefoot runner* © iStockphoto.com/redmal
Photos on pages 154 and 176 by Jennifer Hoffman

Printed in Canada

Rocky Mountain Books acknowledges the financial support for its publishing
program from the Government of Canada through the Canada Book Fund (CBF)
and the Canada Council for the Arts, and from the province of British Columbia
through the British Columbia Arts Council and the Book Publishing Tax Credit.

 Canadian Patrimoine
Heritage canadien

 Canada Council Conseil des Arts
for the Arts du Canada

 BRITISH COLUMBIA
ARTS COUNCIL
Supported by the Province of British Columbia

This book was produced using FSC®-certified, acid-free paper,
processed chlorine free and printed with vegetable-based inks.

For Jenn

For Rio and Silas

For Dan, J and James

For the Buddha within us all

"Believe nothing, no matter where you read it, or who said it, no matter if I have said it, unless it agrees with your own reason and your own common sense"

—BUDDHA

"The day you let go is the day you are forgiven."

—MICHAEL FRANTI

CONTENTS

Start Again

There is motion in stillness and stillness in motion.

I'm always a little nervous before a long run, because often it hurts. I'm an enthusiastic but not particularly talented runner. Nor am I a particularly good Buddhist. Sometimes Buddhism is uncomfortable too. I don't follow any particular doctrine or school of Buddhism; sometimes days pass and I forget to meditate, and I can't remember half the steps of the Eightfold Path.

Nevertheless, this book is the result of the intersection of two important things in my life – running and meditation – and what they have taught me. Running and meditation have been the two principal means by which I have made inquiries into the nature of my own challenges, and I'd like to share with you what I have learned.

This is a book about karma: the power of our actions and their consequences. It started as a blog posting in

2007 and completes its narrative arc in the autumn of 2012. *My* karma is to share this story.

A year before the first essay in this volume, I left a relationship of eleven years. I had been unfaithful, and deeply depressed, and had briefly considered suicide as a solution. I made bad decisions and people I love dearly were hurt, and from this darkness I was able to start again.

This book's purpose is to help you learn one possible path to end suffering. I will try to be honest with you, and I hope that you will be honest with yourself as you read this book. We all suffer; we feel pain and despair that we can't often explain. We also feel joy and bliss, and that provides us with an opportunity to understand the true nature of life and bring an end to our own distress.

A note about style: because these posts were written as blog entries, and not as a concise book of short essays, they vary in structure. Some were penned in the present tense and others in the past. I've chosen to maintain that arrangement to preserve the original tone of each piece.

This book is a snapshot of my life over a six-year period, and because it has a beginning and an end, it may seem as if the journey is somehow complete. It isn't. Even as I write these words I struggle with everything I have learned. I find myself constantly starting again. But that is part of the path to freedom from suffering.

I hope that what I have to say will be of some help to you. Sometimes it feels as though we are moving forward and sometimes we feel as if we're standing still: motion in stillness; stillness in motion. Both are part of the journey. Let's begin.

– Canmore, Alberta

PART ONE

Lacing Up

Take a deep breath. Close your eyes. See yourself running through the woods, up over rocky terrain, and striding out across the summit of a gracefully arcing ridge, or down along the seashore. You are strong and swift.

In 2007 I had just moved into a hundred-year-old house in Fernwood, a funky yet rough-around-the-edges neighbourhood in Victoria, BC. I was living alone for the first time in more than a decade. I was newly single and taking care of my two boys – Rio, who was five, and Silas, not yet two – half-time. I was working at my strategy and communications business, and writing books.

I was running a lot and was determined to embrace a meditation practice as part of a new model of emotional self-care. I was making progress in addressing my anger, and its root cause, fear.

And I met Jenn.

THREE SIMPLE THINGS

I had a conversation with a friend the other night, and in a seemingly casual way she asked, "What are the three things that you would really like to have more of in your life?"

I'm not sure if Jenn was expecting me to say something profound or pedestrian. We were cooking dinner in the Fernwood house, which I'd moved into only a few months before, and part of me was thinking that what I really needed was some basic furniture and maybe a decent wok. Jenn could not have known it at the time, but I'd been contemplating such an enquiry for months, maybe years. Basically I want three simple things: bliss, abundance and love.

A year before this conversation, I had separated from my partner of eleven years, Kathleen. I'd had an affair, which also came crashing to a halt a few months previous, and now I was a single parent, taking care of my two boys – Rio, five, and Silas, a year-and-a-half – while trying to put my life back together. It would be more difficult than I could imagine, and trying to answer that seemingly innocuous question only made the journey more difficult. If all I really wanted was a new couch, I could go and buy one.

While blanching asparagus and grating ginger, Jenn

and I talked about my three simple desires. Bliss, as I have come to think of it, is both a mental and spiritual practice, as well as a physical experience for me. Bliss is a state of being that I experience when I am able to transcend the illusory boundaries that separate me from the rest of the world. Over the last year I had started to experience this more and more.

The feeling is like that of being washed with cold fire. It begins in my chest, just below my heart, and courses through my gut and my torso, down my arms and legs, up through the crown of my head, out the tips of my fingers and through the base of my feet into the earth. At its peak, the experience is like being the sun, but rather than feeling as if I were on fire, I feel like I'm being doused in cool, refreshing water on a hot day.

During the experience, I feel as though I can see 360 degrees around me. Sight is not limited to my eyes. My experience of the world transcends my five primary senses. I don't see *less* when feeling bliss, I see *everything*. I experience the world with my heart, and for fleeting moments feel what avatars have been telling us for millennia, and what quantum physicists have been confirming for the last half-century: everything is one.

This experience of bliss comes most often when I am writing. I'll be typing away at the computer, feeling as through the story I am penning is being written *through* me rather than by me, and then I feel as though I disappear. Sometimes I write through it, letting it speed my fingers on the keyboard. Sometimes it's so intense that I stop and press my palms to my desk and allow bliss to flow through me.

I've felt it walking down the street in my new Fernwood neighbourhood, the sun warming my face. I've felt it during meditation, when I am able to momentarily push thoughts aside and experience pure emptiness. While running one of the rocky trails that are my haunt, I've felt it approaching and willed it forward, inviting it to speed me along the trail, carrying me as if I had Hermes's winged shoes.

When I am able to embrace the day-to-day challenges, I have felt it with my children as I serve them pancakes at the dining room table, or sing along to a Jim Cuddy song in the car.

Jenn listens as dinner nears completion. I tell her that for much of my life I have felt that I don't deserve to succeed. This is different than saying "I deserve to fail." I have believed that I should only come *close* to success, but not actually achieve it. Somewhere in my heart there is a fear of what success means, and that has kept me from achieving what I want to attain in my life: the love of family and friends; love in a romantic relationship; deep and meaningful service through my work; the actualization of my purpose in life as a writer. In short: abundance.

Over the last year I've had to recreate the central story of my life. A year ago, just before Kat and I separated, I hit my nadir. My disasters were all of my own making, but they were disasters nevertheless. I was unhappy in my relationship, and instead of trying to fix the problems, I went looking elsewhere. I had an affair, and while I felt cared for, I also felt an overwhelming sense of despair. I was trapped by my decisions, and for a while the only way I thought I could break free was suicide. On a bright summer day, while running through the sunny woods of Victoria's Mount Doug Park, I began to plan how I would take my own life.

It was then that I realized how badly I needed to start over. So I started over. A central part of that reboot was rethinking how I considered success.

Over the last year I have told myself again and again: I deserve success. We all do. The universe wants us to succeed. God, Jesus, the Tao, Buddha, the myriad Hindu gods, and all the other avatars can be collaborators in our achievements.

With this shift has come a willingness to accept success, and what it means: responsibility, hard work, patience, discipline, and the creation of abundance in my life.

Jenn asks what I mean by abundance. I tell her that for me it means a profusion of love, an abundance of joy, of peace, of freedom from suffering, of happiness, of good health and well-being. It means an abundance of wealth too. Money is simply a *representation* of the exchange of energy in the world. If I can be present in the world with love, with joy, with peace, and in good health and well-being, and bring those things as an act of service to those I work with, then financial success is sure to follow. This is not about growing wealthy at the expense of another; it is finding abundance and success in collaboration with those I serve.

Dinner is ready and I present it at the sparse dining room table in the nearly empty house. Jenn is a patient listener, and our conversation continues during our meal.

Bliss and abundance lead naturally to love. Love is the fundamental force of the universe, and it creates life. Love is pure energy, the force of life that gives form to all matter in the universe and gives rise to our experience of connection to all things, be they mountains or oceans, our lovers or our children. Humankind has evolved to experience this love in a very unique and important way.

When I am in bliss, the boundary between me and the world evaporates. This is pure love. All life is the expression of the universe's yearning for form, for substance, for expression. When I experience myself as a part of the universe, rather than separate from it, it becomes natural to attract abundance into my life.

For me to love in the way I dream possible, I will have to work through the barriers I have created for myself. Anger, impatience and fear all stand as obstacles. Despite the changes I've started to make in my life, I've barely begun to address these impediments to my personal progress. Each of these is, however, an opportunity for spiritual alchemy that can lead to a deeper, more profound experience of the world.

Our conversation goes on long into the night. As we talk, I'm experiencing bliss through my connection to this woman across the table from me. I'm not ready to fall in love. Things are still too raw. I can't help but feel the pull of attraction, but tomorrow Jenn leaves for her home in Alberta, and I wonder when I will see her again.

We finish our dinner and do the dishes, and while we're putting my meagre cookware away, I decide that in addition to those three simple things – bliss, abundance and love – I'd still very much like a new wok.

DREAMING FREEDOM

I've started a daily practice of meditation. Meditation is how I balance the equation with running; it is the stillness that creates some equilibrium in all my frenetic motion. For two decades I've practiced Tai Chi, finding solace in its gentle motion to calm my mind and cool the fire of my anger and impatience. My hope is that meditation will further douse the flames of fear and help me create some semblance of order in my life. I set my alarm early and rise before Rio and Silas do and make a cup of tea. Once awake I find a comfortable place to sit and practice a simple form of meditation that focuses on drawing in and gently releasing my breath. The idea is to remain present, clear of thoughts and at peace.

For the last year, I've come to recognize my anger, and its root cause – fear – to be my greatest barrier to success, and meditation is one way of stripping away the layers so I can confront what I am afraid of and maybe achieve some freedom from the suffering that afflicts me.

Doesn't that sound lovely? If only I could just sit still for thirty minutes a day and attain a state of nirvana –freedom from illusions – life would be great. But there are obstacles. This morning's meditation session was turbulent. They are all pretty turbulent. In the thirty minutes I sat, I spent ten minutes fantasizing about the future, ten minutes replaying old fears and failures, and ten minutes struggling to stay fully present. I've read that if I do this, I can catch a glimpse of my soul. So far, no sightings. There were some dancing lights the other day, and I have experienced the feeling I describe as bliss a couple of times. I've also fallen asleep once or twice.

During my sit this particular morning, I was startled to hear, as clear as a bell, a voice yelling "NO!" inside my head. It was my own voice. I struggled to merely observe this, as I've been taught, and then move past it to try and slip into the gap between thoughts again. But with the voice came a flood of images of my children, and the fear I harbour about losing them as a consequence of my separation from Kat.

Meditation is a portal through which one walks into a room of silence and empty space, where there is no place to hide.

I was deeply relieved when the buzzer went off in the kitchen and I could open my eyes. I was sitting in the sunroom of my Fernwood home, and as is my habit read a sutra – a simple statement designed to provoke an emotional response – from Deepak Chopra's lovely book *The Spontaneous Fulfillment of Desire*. The stanza was: "Imagine that you have left behind forever any sense of anger or resentment." I burst into tears.

For most of my life I have been coiled in anger. The pain of it has plagued me since my earliest memories. As a child I remember listening to my parents fight and tearing things off my wall to get their attention. In high school I started putting my fist through things – doors, windows – out of frustration. Now I lash out, screaming at those I love the most, expressing some fear that I can hardly name, but must in order to free myself of it.

Imagining that I might leave my fear and anger behind forever was too good to believe. I closed my eyes and thought about how it would feel to shed its clutching grip as a snake sheds its skin. I let that feeling pulse through my body, and out into the wider world.

The path toward freedom is not easy. I'm constantly stubbing my toe on rocks and roots in the tangled darkness. But dreaming of this freedom from anger and fear, and imagining it becoming part of the fabric of my waking life, is an incentive to sit again each morning. Without such freedom, there cannot be bliss and there cannot be love.

WORKING IT OUT

It's a perfect spring afternoon: warm enough to work up a sweat while I burn through some issues that have vexed me this week. I drive to Mount Work, north of Victoria on the Saanich Peninsula, and limber up in the parking lot, trying to convince myself that I'm not running up hills as a form of castigation, but rather as a means of self-exploration. It almost works.

I hit the trail hard and curse myself when I reach the first strenuous climb and my legs rebel against the effort. Up the first grade of exposed stone through the dark woods, and then a set of steep switchbacks, I focus on running in a fluid motion. Sometimes when I'm running over tough terrain, I try to imagine that I am water moving over the landscape. It's harder when I'm going uphill.

It's been a hard week. There was one really tough day that has given me a lot to work through, and I'm hammering up this trail in part to let my body sort through my conundrums.

My fear of all the external forces that have control over my happiness has caught up with me this week. Often I allow external approval and external power to rule my emotional state. If things are going well with my children, or if I have a rewarding experience serving a client, then I'm happy.

When I feel threatened, if others exert power over me, if the things I want in life are in danger, I feel emotionally unbalanced. If the cash is running low or I feel lonely and isolated, then I am miserable. In the past, this has led me to deep depressions that have at times been dangerous.

What I want is to view the world through "self-referral," where I am in control of my emotional state. The opposite of this is "object-referral," where external forces control my happiness.

Three things happened in rapid succession on Tuesday of this week that brought this duality into sharp relief: I thought I might lose my home, I worried I might be losing my children, and my love life was thrown into chaos, again.

On Tuesday some friends and I looked at the two adjacent properties to the Fernwood home I am currently renting, with an eye to purchasing all three. My landlord has made no secret of his desire to sell the homes, and it has left me feeling threatened. The hundred-year-old houses are all on a single lot, making them an anomaly in Victoria, and a zoning nightmare. The middle home is a dump and would take a lot of cash, and a lot of work, to make it livable. One of my friends felt suddenly overwhelmed by her busy life, and opted out. The idea fell apart.

The woods begin to thin as I run upward. In places, the dark forest opens into groves of arbutus, their elephantine trunks worn smooth, their sturdy roots clutching the ancient bedrock. I keep the pressure on, running hard up the steep track.

That same evening I picked up Rio, along with Andy, Kat's new man, and we went to see *Harry Potter and the Order of the Phoenix*. Rio and Silas had stayed at my place the night before, and they were supposed to stay with me after the movie, but things didn't work out that way. Little Silas fell asleep at Kat's place while Rio, Andy and I were at the movie, and when we got back, Rio said that he wanted to stay at his mom's too.

I quickly accepted this. What's the point of fighting with a five-year-old who is half-asleep? The hardest thing for both Kathleen and me about our separation has been to let go of seeing our children on a daily basis. Being able to release my intense desire to have my boys with me for more than a night at a time was a Herculean effort of will. By the time I got home, I was feeling quite despondent. I called and talked with Andy to make sure that he and Kat knew that I was simply "going with the flow" by leaving the boys, and not dumping them because I didn't want them around. Andy told me he knew that, and then told me I was "a good man" for being able to accept the change in circumstances. That helped. It's the beginning of a new friendship that we're both very proud of.

Now the woods give way to a bald dome of rock. The trail can be seen as a patch of lighter-coloured stone against the dark hump. This is easy running, and the sweeping view makes it all the more pleasurable.

Later that night I received an email from Jenn. Since our dinner a few weeks ago, we'd been corresponding and chatting, building an intense connection. But like me, she's gone through a break-up in the last year, and is feeling overwhelmed. In the note she said she wasn't sure if she and I could be together. With so many changes in both of our lives, and our living in different provinces, she's feeling overwhelmed and uncertain.

It was a triple blow, and thinking about it as I cross the sun-dappled flank of Mount Work, I am amazed that one of my clients didn't call to tell me that the money had run out too, just so that I would have the opportunity to face all my insecurities at once.

It's obvious to me that each of these challenges was driven by fear: of not having a place to live, where I can care for my children and have a space for creativity, for friends and family; fear of being without my children; fear of being alone.

The root of all these fears is that of being separate from all that surrounds me, and feeling the searing absence of the divine.

Fear creates insecurity. I have been enslaved by fear for most of my life, and I'm sick and tired of it. I want my happiness to be dependent on nothing that is outside my Self. Of course, the Self isn't merely contained by the seemingly linear sack of skin, bones, muscle and tissue called The Body. It's much more than that.

In my finest moments, I am connected by the pulse of life to all things, all beings. When I am fearful, I am not. When I am fearful, I feel a constriction in my chest. My shoulders close in. I feel the thread of white light that connects me with those I love being constrained as my heart retracts to protect me from harm. The feeling of bliss is not possible when I guard my heart this way.

I reach the summit and realize that I've started to tear down those barriers that separate me from the world around me, seeing them for the illusions that they are. I breeze over the summit and down the far side of the mountain to the opposite parking lot, and then turn around and run back up again. I need the time and the physical strain to clear my head and sort through all these challenges.

The three challenges I faced last Tuesday all seem to stem from my struggle to manage every element of my life, and from my fear of losing control. But all these things – my domicile, my children, my love life – are beyond my power. Relinquishing control and being open to spontaneity, to the possibilities that each rich, magical moment brings, is part of the path that I am running. Every moment is a step deeper into the mysteries of life.

The trail on the north side of Mount Work is gloriously steep, and in places I'm using the slick trunks of arbutus to pull myself up the rocky track. Then I'm back on the summit; its rock-strewn promenade is open to the horizon of hills, ocean and sky that makes living on the west coast a daily delight.

It's getting dark, and as the sun sets I glide through the dusky woods, running over the difficult terrain on instinct. Being open to life's mystery means sometimes having to run in the dark. Experiencing the bliss of connection to all things helps me confront my fear and embrace my need to feel in control.

Where will I live, how will my children be present in my life, will I love another soul? If I can truly root my confidence of my own spirit, then regardless of what life presents I will be capable of embracing it with joy, and finding bliss in every moment.

DOES IT LOVE ME?

Kat, Silas, Rio and I recently ventured to China Beach, an hour-and-a-half north of Victoria along the Strait of Juan de Fuca. Though Kat and I have been separated for a year now, we've made a commitment to spend time together with our children. We had an amazing day, with love and friendship between us all – something I'm sure many separated and divorced couples wish they could have.

China Beach is long and sandy, with a sweeping view of the open ocean beyond the protection of the Olympic Peninsula. Waves pound this shoreline harder than they do the beaches closer to Victoria, giving it a wilder feeling. The sun beat down as Rio and Silas and I dug holes and erected beach logs in them, creating a row of wooden towers from the tide line down into the sea. Kat swam in the ocean.

One of the many highlights of the day was a moment toward the end of the afternoon when Rio, his keen eye always roving for details, found a tiny beetle in the sand. He gently picked it up and spent a good ten minutes examining it, allowing it to crawl over his hands and arms, looking at it from every possible angle. Finally he looked at me and asked, "Does it love me?"

My first thought was, no, of course not, it's a beetle; it

doesn't experience love. But I considered this a moment before saying anything. All my life I've been thinking about love; never more so than in the last year. I finally said: "Yes, it does love you. You and the beetle are made up of the same fabric of the universe. And that fabric is bound together by the energy of love. You and the beetle, and everything else, for that matter, are all connected in a way we can only catch fleeting glimpses of."

That seemed to satisfy Rio, because next he asked if he could give the beetle a corn chip.

I've been thinking about Rio's question – about love, not the corn chip – ever since. Implicit in the statement was that Rio loved the beetle. On its own, I find that impossibly beautiful. That I have raised children who feel capable of love for nature, for creation, for the "other," is beyond my wildest dreams.

But my astonishment goes deeper than that. I think of people, and everything else in the world, as ripples in the sea of the universe, like the waves pounding off the shore of China Beach. All existence is an ocean, and we are individual waves; temporary and unique, but invariably a part of one another. The boundaries between ourselves and the life around us are imaginary, like the boundary between waves on the sea.

At the subatomic level, looking deep into the core of all matter, nothing is solid. All physical form – me, you, the desk I sit at to write, the beetle on Rio's arm – is made up of materials that are almost exclusively nothing. You and I are made mostly of water, and water is 99 percent empty space. The nuclei of the atoms that make up water are surrounded by an electron clouds that are nearly entirely void of matter. We look and feel solid, but that's only in comparison to the space that surrounds us. In reality, we're composed almost entirely of nothing at all. When seen this way, the boundaries between us virtually disappear.

But this isn't very practical. If we actually saw the world this way, there would be chaos. We'd have been eaten by sabre-toothed tigers before we could invent fire; instead of seeing a fuzzy wave-like thing with big teeth, we see danger. This view of the world is the product of sensory perception attuned not for total understanding, but for culturally driven minimalism. Simply stated, our senses aren't attuned to see, hear and feel the universe as it must really be, because its complexity is so vast that we would likely go blitheringly mad trying to live our strange, material lives. We see the boundaries between us not because they are real, but because we have to see them or we'd never get through a single day. It doesn't mean we can't learn to *feel* the universe as it actually is. Love is how we experience this reality.

Love is the energy that connects my wave to yours; my wave to Rio's and Silas's; and their waves to the beetle's. Love is the portal through which we slip together into a more perfect understanding of what our world, our universe, really is, where boundaries between one life and the next are fuzzy waves more than rigid lines.

So yes, my dear boy, the beetle loves you, just as you love it. And yes, I'm certain beyond a doubt it would like a corn chip.

SOCKS

I'm working on a mathematical equation for a probability theory I've got rattling around in my head. So far the equation looks like this: $X = Y (A{\times}B)C^2$.

Whereas X is the likelihood that I will be able to get the children completely dressed in under an hour, Y is the item of clothing that I am trying to find for one of the children (underwear, a clean pair of pants, a shirt that isn't too big or too small, a pair of socks, any pair of socks, I don't even care if they are matching anymore), A is the number of trips the children have taken back and forth between my home and Kat's, B is the likelihood that on any given day Rio has chosen or been forced to wear underwear when he went out the door, and C is the size of the pile of unfolded laundry on the floor in the closet of the boys' room. The squared part is just to make it look more mathematical.

The other evening, I was labouring to get the boys out the door to pick up my mother at the airport – something that they were both admittedly excited to do – and I was stymied. I found one pair of underwear for Rio, and after some cajoling convinced him that he should put it on *before* his pants. But the only pair of pants in the whole house that I would let him go out the door in were two sizes too big. The other two pairs were both ratty-looking track pants, which he prefers, but I wouldn't allow him to step into the world wearing them even if it meant keeping him home from school. And yes: more than once, to my horror, he has shown up at my house after a day at school with them on.

I found one of my belts and managed to cinch it down to his slender waist, and that did the trick. So Rio was dressed. Then it was Silas's turn. The pants that I had, when held up for closer inspection, were grubby with ground-in grime on the knees and covered in purple stains of various kinds – paint, juice, blackberries. I flung them across the room. How could I not have gotten these clean in the bazillion washes they'd gone through? Finally I settled on the least stained of my options, and got a cute T-shirt on Silas's hefty frame to distract from the abysmal state of his bottoms.

Then I went to find a pair of socks.

In the Pixar animated film *Monsters, Inc.*, one monster returns from a child's room – where he is doing his job scaring the bejesus out of sleeping children – with a sock on his back, and trips the contamination alarm. It seems that the monsters fear children as much as children fear monsters. Children, their toys, clothing, and especially their socks are considered toxic. When the monster returns through the closet-door portal to his own world with the sock clinging to his back, he is shaved to the hide and given decontamination shower. The sock returns again and again throughout the movie. Pixar story creators *must* have kids. There are miniature socks all over my house. I find them in the couch. In the cupboards. In the bathroom. In my bed. Out in the car. I dutifully round them up and wash them and put the mismatched socks on a shelf in the boys' room to wait for their errant matches to emerge from some dusty corner of the house. Sometimes they do; most often they don't.

A few weeks ago I sent a bag of socks to Kat's place. It was her idea. There were about thirty mismatches in it. Kat told me that she had a similar collection at her own home, and that she'd sort them out. The next time I had the boys at my place, they came with a bag full of matched socks. It was lovely. It lasted two weeks! Now, as I crawled around in the walk-in closet in their room, searching for socks, my mother's plane likely already on the tarmac, I could scarcely come up with two that fit Silas, let alone two of the same colour.

Frustrated, I picked up the phone and called Kat. My old pattern is to blame others. But I am trying to forge a new relationship with Kat, and a new approach to my frustrations, so instead of illogically blaming her for something that the laws of thermodynamics and quantum physics combined couldn't puzzle out, I commiserated with her.

Kat is far more relaxed about these things. She thinks the sweatpants that I want to light on fire and bury in the back yard are cute. Underwear isn't a big deal. I'm a *little* more uptight. We talk about it. I have permission to burn the pants if I want, but I won't, because Rio adores them.

Rio, Silas and I get out the door. I can chalk up another lesson learned: don't get to attached to anything: an idea, a way of presenting yourself to the world. Not even a pair of socks.

TRAIL NOTES: PART ONE

What are you afraid of?

When you are angry or afraid, what can you do to
express it without hurting yourself or anyone else?

Who are you blaming for the things in your
life that haven't gone as you planned?

What do you think is underneath – at
the root – of your fear?

What stories do you have to give up to be happy?

PART TWO

Uphill through Rocks

The first few minutes of most runs are easy. Then the trail becomes steep; there are roots and rocks, and my legs turn to cement and my head fills with voices. Sometimes it's a punch in the gut, but I keep running.

Meditation is the same. My back gets sore, my legs ache from being crossed, and sometimes the din in my head is deafening.

Run through it; sit through it.

The initial effort to address my own suffering led to a false summit. It was illusion. But every footfall along the trail was a step forward.

The children were with me three nights a week in our home in Fernwood. The pain of being away from Rio and Silas the other four was acute in those first two years after separation. I ran to make sense of things.

My second book, a mystery novel called *The Cardinal Divide*, was accepted for publication.

And I fell in love. And it was complicated.

GOD IN THE HILLS

There are seventy switchbacks between the trailhead and our first camp on Phillips Ridge, high in Strathcona Provincial Park, on Vancouver Island. Even though I had lived in Victoria for two-and-a-half years, this hike with my best friend, J, was my first foray into the island's rugged interior. It was a wonderful experience to be back in the mountains, lugging a pack up the steep trails, feeling the various pinches and aches and pains that come with self-reliance, but I felt every single one of those switchbacks.

When we were younger, J and I spent nearly every weekend in the backcountry of Banff, Kootenay, Yoho and Jasper National Parks, or in the Front Range peaks and foothills of Kananaskis Country, in Alberta. We logged uncountable miles, partly on trail but mostly off, striding out across the vastness of the Rocky Mountain wilderness.

Our four days in Strathcona were all spent along the convoluted spine of Phillips Ridge. We didn't set any records for distance or heroics. It's unlikely that the *Canadian Alpine Journal* will be asking me to pen something for this year's tome. For me the most remarkable part of the experience was rekindling the memory of how powerful a connection a person can have with God while surrounded by wide open country.

My definition of God has changed dramatically over the last twenty years. I grew up in a quasi-Catholic household where church was reserved for Christmas and Easter, and even then only sporadically. When I was in high school I read the little Gideon version of the Bible nearly every night, turning to its pages for solace during tumultuous times. There were many. By college I had given up on most of what I had read, and when I moved to the mountains in 1992, I discarded the rest, replacing theology with the physical sciences as an explanation for everything I could see, hear, touch and taste. I couldn't perceive then that science, particularly quantum physics, would lead me back to God.

I define God as the sum of all the possibilities that exist in the universe. The universe, according to quantum physicists, is primarily made up of energy and information, hurtling across space at the speed of light, taking form here and there as solar systems, stars, planets, platypuses, people and other unlikely critters. Some physicists argue these days that it is a conscious universe, where matter takes shape with intention, where the thing formed and the will to form it are one in the same.

According to the wave-particle theory in quantum physics, everything exists only as "probability" until you and I see it. Physicists have conducted experiments demonstrating that until a particle is observed, it exists as a wave that holds an infinite number of possibilities. Once it is observed, that wave snaps into a single particle, becoming what we expect it to be. That chair you are sitting on only becomes the familiar form when you observe it. Until then, the particles that make it up are just the probability of a chair.

These things are formed from the energy and information that is connected through what is called "the unified field." This is God's playground. God, the creator, is just another word for conscious possibility. You and I are part of God, consciously creating the unfolding universe, because until we observe it, matter is nothing more than the possibility of the objects we are familiar with. Mind you, it's just a theory. While sitting high on Phillips Ridge, the vastness of nature spread before me, I not only thought about the idea of God but felt it. That's where theory gets put to the test.

The man who would become the Buddha, when he set out to conquer suffering, didn't turn to the crowded cities of ancient India: he went into the wilderness and sat beneath the Bodhi tree. Jesus, after his baptism, went into the wilderness to prepare himself in solitude for the work he was on earth to do. Muhammad first heard God's call to him to become the prophet while alone in the desert. In both the Vedic and Taoist traditions, we are urged to spend time in direct communion with nature in order to see this field of all possibilities. To feel it. To be a part of its consciousness. Through connection with nature's abundance we are able to sense, in our hearts, the magnificence of creation. What we are learning now is that we too are part of that creation. That we too are part of God.

I feel singularly connected with creation when overlooking distant ranges of mountains along the knotted spine of Phillips Ridge. The feeling I have is love. It's not love for something. It's not love for nature. It is simply love of existence, of the inseparability of all things.

"God is love," the Bible says, in 1 John 4:8. That's where it should have ended, before we started talking about "whosoever believeth in him should not perish, but have everlasting life" (John 3:16), which just muddied the waters, and started putting conditions on love. "God will love you if…."

God is love. Period. Love is the energy that binds the universe together. It is what causes creation. We are a part of that love; we are simultaneously its creators and its destiny. When we are in nature, we are simply a little bit more conscious of our part in God, in creation and in the conception of that love.

CROSSING THE DIVIDE

Mountain ranges slip past and the ocean is at my back as I drive toward the Rocky Mountains and over the Continental Divide for the first time in more than two years. The heartache that I am feeling is worse than anything I've ever experienced.

Jenn came to Victoria for work and for some time together, and I've fallen head over heels in love; our week-long visit has gone off the rails as we try to imagine a future together. Now, as planned, I'm driving her home to Canmore, Alberta. Canmore is where I lived with Kat for nearly a decade, and where *her* partner, Andy, still lives. Kat is there visiting with Rio and Silas, and the plan is for me to meet the boys there and spend a few days with them before heading back to BC. It's a mess, and so am I.

Apparently you can't go home again. At least not when you're dragging so much baggage behind you. I cross the height of land that marks the border between BC and Alberta, and separates watersheds east and west, and it's all downhill, figuratively and literally. I come back to the Rockies with such a tangle of emotions that I can scarcely breathe. Driving into the Bow Valley and saying goodbye to Jenn was one of the most painful things I've ever done. I find myself gasping for breath after I drive away.

Canmore holds too many knotted emotions. So,

heartbroken and with the long drive complete, I pick up beer and drive east, determined to skip town and sleep that night away from the place. All the suffering seems too much. Before I make the highway again, a voice rises in me so dire that after I scream, I fear I may have done permanent damage to my vocal cords. And then comes a mournful sound so terrible that I frighten myself with it. The tremors pass and I sleep in a parking lot at a trailhead for the night, curled in my sleeping bag in the back of my Impreza.

Morning arrives and I drive back into town to pick up my boys. I can't contain my tears when I embrace them. Rio puts his hands on my face and Silas climbs over me, his face aglow. They are the love of my life. Letting go of my children was the one thing I said I couldn't do when Kat and I separated, and now I've done it, though only for short spells. Kat and Andy are both very supportive and I realize what my partner of eleven years and I have now is so much better than what we did when we were a couple. It doesn't erase the pain of having left so much behind, but it helps.

The boys and I beat it out of town and hit the Calgary Zoo and spend the day there. It's magical being back with my kids, so much so that my anguish fades to a dull ache for periods of an hour at a time. At one point it bubbles back to the surface (after watching a male and female lion playfully bite each other's ears: I'm a sucker for romance) and I find myself leaking tears while fixing a snack for Rio. I tell him that my heart is aching. He looks into my reddened eyes and says, "I will sing you a love song." And then, right there in front of the giraffes, he composes this song out of the sweetness of his heart:

> I love you so much
> I love you as big as the sky
> I wanna make your heart heal all up
> I wanna give you a great big hug
> And then, I wanna give you a big kiss.

It's the most beautiful song anybody has ever sung me. We write the lyrics down and sing them to each other.

It's not the only love song that has been given to me in the last few days. Friends Jason Mogus and Laura McKenzie, whose wedding I will be DJing later in August, have selected "One Step Closer to You," from Michael Franti's album *Yell Fire!* as their first dance, so I've been listening to it a lot in the last few days:

> I let go of my broken heart
> I let go to an open heart
> I let go of my broken dreams
> I let go to the mystery.
> I believe in the miracle
> I believe in the spiritual
> I believe in the one above
> I believe in the one I love.

Silas and Rio and I listen to that song in our Calgary

hotel room that night. As we dance together, Silas wraps his two-year-old arms around me with such vigor that you'd think that the boy knew exactly what the man was feeling. The bands of steel loosen around my chest, and I feel the boundary between him and me evaporate. Even in pain, there is bliss. I experience that sacred moment of connection, and I know that I don't have to hold on to this suffering. I can let go.

There is more than one place to cross the Continental Divide, and the journey is just beginning.

THE PLAIN OF SIX GLACIERS

After two days in Alberta, it feels as if I never left – the place or the clutter of stories I've told myself about who I was and how I should move through this world. Somehow I've slipped back into the belief that I don't deserve success, as easily as I slipped over the Continental Divide a few nights ago. Is it the place or the circumstances?

I rise on Monday morning still reeling. It's time to drown this stupidity in a flash flood of endorphins. After a few days with Rio and Silas, visiting the Calgary Zoo and the Royal Tyrrell Museum, I've dropped them with Kat and Andy in Canmore, and have driven to Lake Louise to visit old friends. I make for the lake itself and start my run along the pan-flat lakeshore.

For five summers and a couple of winters in the early and mid-1990s, Lake Louise was my home. I worked as a naturalist for Parks Canada, leading hikes along the shore of Lake Louise and up the valley beyond, called the Plain of Six Glaciers. I must have tramped into that scene, immortalized on a million postcards, more than a hundred times, but I still consider it one of the finest hikes in the Rockies, with stunning views of the Continental Divide and its glaciers, and only a thousand feet of elevation to gain and a dozen kilometres' round trip for your troubles.

Now, I recall every single one of them and allow myself to settle into the familiar rhythm of trail running.

Running in the mountains feels euphoric, and for more than two hours I nearly forget my foolish troubles. Mountains have a way of doing that: they put our difficulties into perspective. They dwarf our suffering with their stalwart grandeur. As I glide up the trail, it occurs to me that the Stephen running through this primeval landscape is so different from the one who first plodded up this hill; time indeed has slipped away.

I pass the tea house after five kilometres and run out the trail to the Abbot Pass lookout, stepping carefully along the narrow edge of the lateral moraine that drops off two hundred feet to the debris-covered Lower Victoria Glacier. At the lookout I sit alone and feel the sun on my face, feel the pulse of life through my limbs, feel the surge of energy through my system. It's a good thing to be alive on this earth.

The run down is pure bliss. My feet know every step, and my running on the rocky slopes of Mount Doug, Mount Work and the trails in the hills above Thetis Lake has given me good footwork, so I feel as though I am flying.

I spend the rest of the day visiting friends and have dinner at the Lake Louise hostel with Jim and Jack, who I met the very first day I moved to the west. It's good to connect with these men, both of whom are in their sixties, and to be reminded of the arc of time's swift passage.

The passage of time. The belief in my deserving. The faith in my spirit as my central reference point. The ability to love unconditionally. These are the things that crossing the Continental Divide has dredged up. It's not the place really, it's the man. And now, playing a waiting game with love, I try to find the equanimity of self-referral to calm my mind and gently numb the pain in my chest and return again to a place where I know that I deserve to succeed beyond my own wildest imagination.

SIX DRAWINGS

Rio, Silas and I arrive back in Victoria after a fifteen-hour road trip. Kat drove the boys as far as Kamloops, where I met them and carried on homeward. I fought a cold the entire way. For most of my adult life, whenever I've undergone some kind of major emotional challenge, my body works through the trauma by getting good and sick. In the past I'd give in, but now I fight it. I meditate on perfect health and imagine how it feels to be vibrant and full of energy. I refuse to give into sickness: I silently repeat that I am in perfect health and actually create the feeling of wellness inside me. Sometimes I imagine how I feel after a really satisfying run and allow that sensation to permeate my body. This almost always works, but not this time.

I take Silas to daycare, but Rio is set against it (Silas is set against it too, but he is still too small, and lacks the language to mount an effective counter-campaign). I can't blame Rio, so he sticks with me as I try to clean up both the physical and emotional wreckage from the journey. By mid-afternoon I'm beat. I give into the repeated requests by Rio to watch a movie, and he puts on *The Two Towers*, arguing that he really likes the "scary parts." He points out that the Orcs don't brush their teeth, so they become bad guys.

Kat, now back from her trip, comes by for dinner and offers to take the boys for the night so I can rest and recover from my cold. This is the sort of flexibility that she and I are so proud of in our new relationship. When we split up, we made a decision: we would move beyond the pain of our separation and focus on our friendship. I credit Kat with her swift and seemingly easy forgiveness of me for our ability to enjoy this new kinship with our children.

Before they leave, Rio and I settle into the couch to snuggle and watch a bit of the movie together. There is a scene in *The Two Towers* where Aragorn is portrayed as the king, cast in stone after his death, and Arwen, his bride, is seen by his side, mourning his passing. Rio watches and his eyes grow narrow and he turns to me and asks, "Is that what I will look like when I die?"

Oh, boy.

"No," I say. "That's a sculpture of Aragorn. It's a carving that they made of him so people will be able to remember him."

"So what will I look like when I die?"

I choose my words carefully: "After people are *really* sure that we are dead, we are buried under the ground, or we are cremated.

"What's cremated?"

"That's when they put our bodies into a great big oven and turn on some flames and what's left is just ashes.

Then sometimes our ashes are sprinkled over a place we love, like a mountain or the ocean."

Just saying the words makes cremation sound scary. Rio starts to cry, his arms wrapped tightly around my neck. "I don't want to die. I don't want to go into an oven," he says. "I want to be buried." I assure him that it will be many, many years before he dies, and that he gets to choose what happens when he does. I save the cheery news about embalming for some other time.

He looks into my eyes again, his face tracked with tears. "What happens to me after I die?" he asks.

"Our bodies might die and disappear," I tell him, "but our souls, our spirit, remain." I tell him that our bodies contain our organs and our muscles and our blood, but that our souls are what allow us to feel. "Our souls are the conscious energy of the universe, and when we die, that energy returns to the trees, to the birds, to the rocks, the sky, the ocean, and to each other."

"What is a soul for?" Rio asks.

"Our souls allow us to feel. What you are feeling right now," I put my hand on his belly, "this worry about dying," and then I put my hand on his heart, "and the love you feel for Momma and Silas and me, those feelings come from your soul. It allows us to feel joy and sorrow, fear and happiness, loneliness and love."

I tell him that our soul allows our hearts to stay connected with one another because our souls extend beyond our bodies and touch each other even when we are far apart. This seems to satisfy him, because he shows me some of the new scrapes and bruises he's collected in the last few days.

But later, when he touches my tear-streaked face as we say goodbye, he reminds me of the drawings he did for me that afternoon. He's come down from his room to show them to me. We've been playing together, drawing pictures filled with rivers and oceans and coral reefs for the new action figures we picked up at the Calgary Zoo. Rio has half a dozen new drawings in total. He gives them to me with great reverence, saying "Whenever you miss me, when I am at Momma's, or when you are away, you can just look at them, and you will know I love you." I bend down to kiss him goodbye, and he announces, "I will still love you when I die."

I kiss him and cradle his beautiful face in my hands and say, "Of course you will. Love goes on forever. It will never, ever end."

He, Kat and Silas leave, and I trudge upstairs and crawl into bed. I read *The Prophet*, by Kahlil Gibran, from cover to cover, along with a few stories from Barry Lopez's *River Notes*, and an old, sad essay by Edward Abbey. But before sleep comes, I tuck Rio's six drawings under my pillow. They are symbols of pure love, from a boy whose heart is open so wide it casts the most radiant light on all that it touches.

BREAKING THE SHELL

In *The Prophet,* Kahlil Gibran says this of suffering: "Your pain is the breaking of the shell that encloses your understanding."There isn't a single shell, but layers upon layers of shell. We emerge into this world at the centre of these layers, swaddled in our understanding and the endless freedom from suffering some of us seek. That first moment of blissful emergence from the womb is the first shell through which we must break, and it would seem that the rest of our days are preparation for, and emergence through, subsequent layers.

For some. It is no wonder many of us choose to lock ourselves *inside* the shell and placate our inquiry with reality TV, booze, drugs, shopping, general excess, sloth and general malaise – all substitutes for the hard work of genuine growth.

And who can blame us? It is painful. Breaking the shell hurts. As we grow spiritually, we find that the layer of shell that contains us no longer fits, and we press up against it, and when we finally break through, there is discomfort, even pain. Gibran says: "Much of your pain is self-chosen. It is the bitter potion by which the physician within you heals your sick self."

This recent emergence has been among the most painful, and beyond a doubt I know it was self-chosen.

I believed that I had broken the most painful layers of shell when Kat and I separated, but now I'm pressing up against subsequent layers that are resisting fracture.

What am I finding as I break through these layers of shell? I still must work to define my own happiness internally, rather than externally. My happiness must be the result of my own spiritual grounding, and not the people in my life, their approval or acceptance of me, my financial status, whether I have my children with me every day, or what the weather happens to be doing during a rainy Victoria summer. I must continue to affirm that I deserve to succeed in love, in work and in life.

Painful but necessary lessons. Why accept such pain? If I was to choose not to break the shell, but instead to retreat back inside of it, I would die spiritually. With each emergence, the world becomes so much more beautiful, so much more bountiful, so much more magical. It is my purpose to strive to see the world as it really is.

I wonder if it gets easier? Some of the layers of shell that I've broken through have been very painful, but others haven't been as difficult. I remember that first conscious moment when I actually felt, rather than simply imagined, the connectivity of all things, which I think of as bliss: I was practising Tai Chi on the beach at Hollyhock, a retreat centre on remote Cortes Island, between Vancouver Island and the mainland. I slipped out of the confines of my physical self and gently became the sand, the jumble of logs on the foreshore, the water lapping on the high-water mark, the dark forests beyond. I remember walking, as if through a dream, down the beach to find a three-foot-long mud shark on the beach. I knew it was there not because I could see it but because I *was* the beach; I felt it on my sandy back.

That wasn't so painful. Some layers we emerge through in pleasure, and others we have to struggle hard to break. My guess is that as our heart and spirit grow wise along this spiritual journey, each layer will become unique, and our memory of and insight into our past emergence will make the breaking shell softer, and the recovery from its pain faster.

FUCKING WITH MY
FIFTH CHAKRA

Full disclosure right up front: I've not always been gentle with folks who talk of chakras. In fact, I have made good-natured fun of chakra-talk in the past. I've also made fun of the didgeridoo in the past, but then I experienced the didge in all its baritone glory and things changed, but that's another story. My point is this: all that was yesterday, and this is today, and I'm done putting my thinking in a box simply because I can't see or feel or touch something with my own dim-witted senses.

So let's talk chakras. There are seven, and they extend up the body, starting at the base of the spine, and ending at the very top of the head (or just above the crown, according to some). Chakras are the body's energy centres, where the physical and spiritual self intersect. They are internal portals through which we pass on life's journey.

Recently I made a mess of my fifth chakra. It is in the area of the throat and is the centre for communication and creativity. It is the portal from the lower chakras, which focus on the body, into the realm of mind and spirit. This chakra's element is air, and it is associated closely with sound. Sound of course is vibration, and vibrate is what every speck of matter — every wave and particle of energy and information in the universe – does all the time.

When I was in Canmore and leaving Jenn, I screamed "fuck" so loud, so harshly, with such despair and fury, that at the time I was certain I had damaged my larynx. It was a release of the pent-up energy, anger, frustration, fear, pain and regret that I hadn't been able to express during the almost unimaginable drive from Victoria to Alberta. It came out all at once. Twelve hours – maybe twelve years – of emotion, rushing out, making one hell of a vibration. Moments later, before turning onto the high- way, I had to pull over to sob pitifully, another release of despair that had never fully emerged in the last year.

But the next day, and the day after that, my throat was fine. I was worn thin, and weary, but my throat was as well as the rest of me. Then I caught a what I thought was a cold, and it settled in my throat. The pain in my throat became severe; the only way I could eat was to swallow half-a-dozen Motrin or more a day. When the flu symptoms never materialized but the sore throat con- tinued, I remembered "the scream."

The fifth chakra is about self-expression, about speak- ing the truth, about letting go of constrictions and expec- tations. What I felt most acutely over the ten days starting with the drive to Alberta was an utter inability to say what I meant, and explain how I really felt, to someone who I cared for. I felt during that time that I simply could not express my true self, that I could not open my heart.

Then the shroud that blanketed my self-expression lifted, and my throat healed. What I had to do was let go. To become, as the Buddhist nun Pema Chödrön says, "comfortable with uncertainty." Let go of needing to know what tomorrow might bring. It was a way of being truthful, because the ultimate reality is uncertainty and complete vulnerability.

I spent a lot of time in meditation during these challenging few weeks. I would imagine my throat bathed in white light. During the fleeting moments of clarity I had during these silent experiences, one image continued to appear in my mind: my throat gently opening, my head tilting back toward the sky, my eyes closed, while a dove emerged from the naked space of my neck, the sky-blue light of the fifth chakra spilling from the fissure as the bird took flight.

NO ILLUSIONS ON
JOCELYN HILL

There's no place to hide when you're grinding up seven kilometres of steep, rocky trail.

The number of illusions that I surround myself with every day of my existence is staggering. The illusion of the past, the innumerable stories I've created about who I have been, and how I became who I am today. Most of what I remember is erroneous. If something happened more than a year ago, the likelihood of my remembering it with any accuracy, or recounting it with any veracity, is slim. It's illusion.

The illusion of the future, the scenarios that play out in my head about the days, weeks and months to come, are even less likely. Tomorrow is a mystery, next week impossible to imagine with precision. And yet I spend vast amounts of time, and huge amounts of emotional energy, allowing the dreamscape of tomorrow to dominate my present.

Jocelyn Hill is a good grind for working through illusions. It's the high point of Gowlland Tod Provincial Park, on the Saanich Peninsula, north of Victoria. As I start up the long, steep incline, I look down at my feet picking their way over stones and roots. Breathing hard, feeling the burn of lactic acid in my legs, I bury myself in illusions, anything to avoid the present. Because the present is sweat, throbbing muscles, tearing lungs. The conflict is obvious: I know I live in a world of illusions, but I'm trying to strip them away.

The day, which only moments ago was threatening rain, has become sunny, and as legs and lungs fall into a rhythm, I realize I've not been actually seeing the green world around me for the last kilometre. I'm missing the present by living in the illusions in my head.

This is the only reality; this is as real as it gets. Right now. I struggle with my illusions all the way to the summit, seven kilometres and a thousand feet up from the trailhead. When I make the rocky dome, I continue, circling back via a route that inspires me with views down, down, down to the Saanich Inlet far below, and to the green hills far in the distance.

On the flight down, shirt off, sweat stinging my eyes, the wet leaves and branches whipping my body, I contemplate again the notion of illusions. Getting lost in the illusion of past and future pulls me away from my centre. Illusions distract me from my goal of grounding my own happiness internally. Illusions create stories about my past, they call my ego to the fore and allow me to act out scenarios for the future. Staying focused on the present moment, the trail drilling past me, the scent of wet leaves perfuming the morning, the crispness of the air on my flesh, the feeling of my feet light on the rocks and bald roots: these things keep me centred. These things keep me aware of my own soul, and its connection to all that surrounds me. They also keep me from tripping and falling on my face.

Two hours and fifteen minutes after setting out, I am back at my car. I have no illusions that the lessons learned on Jocelyn Hill will need to be relearned.

THE FRACTAL EQUATION
FOR BEACH GLASS

Fractal Equation, noun: a geometric pattern than is
repeated at every scale and so cannot be represented
by classical geometry.

The sky presses close to the shore when Silas, Rio and I
trip down to Clover Point in Victoria for a Sunday afternoon gallivant. Silas is asleep in my arms as we make our
way over the rocks and logs. Rio, armed to the teeth with
swords and a Power Ranger's spear (early Halloween
custom accessories) deftly navigates the obstacles. Silas
continues his sleep wrapped in a fleece blanket, while
Rio and I bat rocks with flat pieces of driftwood, a favourite beach pastime. But that grows dull, and Rio asks
for a new game.

I'm stumped. I'm on my knees, picking up dollar-sized
stones to whack, and instead of rising and knocking them
out to sea, I dig a little deeper. I find a speck of clear beach
glass, polished and wet, just under the top layer of stones.
Rio says it looks like a jelly bean, and speculates on its
flavour: popcorn. I push a few more rocks aside and find
another one, and another. Soon I've dropped the fistful of
stones I had collected, and Rio and I are pushing layers

of beach rocks aside, finding dozens of tiny brown, blue, green, white and even red specks of glass.

I've spent a lot of time on the beach, but I'm rarely the one who brings home the big find. My good friend Jack could walk along any stretch of beach and find something extraordinary: half a dozen Japanese fishing floats, a Pepsi bottle from the 1940s, a glass eye from a sixteenth-century pirate, something that he lost in Baja California in 1969. I once found a hockey glove at Cape Scott, the northern tip of Vancouver Island. I think it may have been part of a load of such items washed off a container ship somewhere far out in the Pacific. I left it on the beach for others to enjoy. That's about it.

So finding such a wealth of beach glass under my feet in a place that I visit often (three times this week, for example) is nothing short of amazing.

Of course, it's always been there. It reminded me that the scale at which nature presents marvels is infinite: it's fractal.

Silas sleeps while Rio and I excavate. Rio thoughtfully puts up barriers to keep the tide from washing over our prone bodies. In an hour my pockets are full and we're on to filling our Frisbee.

For an hour Rio and I are absorbed in our task. I think of little else. He dances, waves his arms like a maniac, builds barriers, laughs when my shoes got soaked because I'm not paying attention and comes dutifully to inspect each piece of glass I deem worthy of his perusal.

I keep saying to him, "This glass is always under our feet, like a secret treasure buried just beneath the surface." He keeps on dancing. I've learned it's pretty hard to feel down when you're dancing.

The fractal essence of nature's marvels, its patterns, its gifts, make me think of a conversation with my friend Dan Spinner late in the week. Dan has been my business – and life – coach for several months now. We were talking about some of the intense lessons I've been learning, and relearning, over the last while. He reminded me that these lessons were fractal: that when learned in one area of my life, they could be repeated in many others. The lessons I've learned around success in work, therefore, could be applied to the recent conflagration in my love life, and in raising my kids. First we have to see the pattern behind the lesson.

My pattern? To fear uncertainty, rather than embracing it as a given in life. I want so badly to believe that everything good will last forever and everything bad will disappear the instant I feel it. But nothing in life is assured; every moment is a step into the unknown. That's why, when you find beach glass right under your feet, the only thing you can do is dance.

RUNNING TOWARD
STILLNESS

It's a welcome sunny day in the autumn, and J and I park his car at the Pike Road entrance to East Sooke Park, and then drive mine south to Aylard Farm to start our run. I don't get nervous at the start of a long run anymore: I know I can do this. I don't fear the physical discomfort that might come. Instead, I'm exhilarated by the prospect of moving through the coastal landscape at the southernmost tip of Vancouver Island on this extraordinary day.

We begin along the path slowly, warming up, falling into a rhythm of conversation and an easy flow along the gravel trail to the beach. The midday sunshine gleams off the swells, and the beach is strewn with bull kelp as we follow the water's edge. The tide is high, so we scramble up the bank and into the woods along some of the most exquisite seashore on this part of Vancouver Island.

The path winds through groves of naked arbutus trees and over rocky outcrops. This is the sort of running where you use your hands a lot, pulling up steep cliffs and dropping down over rocky abutments. Below us, sometimes a hundred feet or more down sheer rock walls, the surf pounds the exposed southern point of the island, its roar omnipresent, filling the space around us with a cacophony of white noise.

We pass Beechey Head, warming up. I can feel my body starting to intuit the trail, my mind relaxing into the run. Our conversation takes long pauses as we pound up steep sections of the trail that climb high above the sea, where finger inlets poke the rocky bulkheads. Then down again, through thick mats of salal.

Every step forward is a step into joy. Every step forward is a step into bliss.

In the last two or three years, trail running has become the yang component of my body/spirit workout. I've been running all my life, but never like this. I was a skinny kid who was frequently chided for his lack of athletic prowess. In grade four I was on my school's cross-country team. I didn't run much during grade school, except through the woods behind my home in Burlington, where second-growth maple, pine and beech cast dark pools of cool shadow during the heat of Southern Ontario summers. In high school and college I dated a woman who was a track and field athlete, and she inspired me to run again.

It wasn't until moving to the Rockies in 1992 that I ran again with any regularity. When I landed at the western edge of the continent two-and-a-half years ago, I replaced Nordic skiing with cross-country running as the mainstay of my workout. It is the fastest pathway I know to bliss.

J and I race down a long, muddy slope to where the

trail crosses a rocky beach and a sheltered cove just south of Cabin Point. From here the trail climbs steeply up through jagged buttresses of stone and more tangled forest to emerge on a broad, open plateau a few hundred feet above the crashing tide. This is my favourite place on the Coast Trail: this flat expanse of stone and meadow where I can stride out and feel the contentment of a cadence with land, sea, sky, muscle and heart.

Just a few weeks ago I ran to Cabin Point and back on my own, shaking off another difficult parting from Jenn. We keep trying to make things work, and so far we keep falling short. But within us is the spark of recognition that in each other we have found the missing half of our own souls, so we keep trying. I remember crossing this bench wishing that I was not alone, that she was there to share this miraculous place with me.

J and I push ourselves along the trail, feeling the effortless flow that comes at the apex of a run. I know that soon I'll touch, however briefly, the stillness that I am seeking in all my efforts.

Running is the motion component of the equation; meditation is the stillness. But there is stillness in motion and motion in stillness. From time to time I am jolted from sitting by an urge to move. To escape my mind. I lurch from my cushion and have to gently remind myself to "sit through" whatever is making me so uncomfortable. The urge to run, during these challenging times, is almost overwhelming.

This is where yin and the yang create not opposites playing against one another but two halves of a whole, becoming one.

When I run, I allow my mind to range over the landscape. The technical nature of most of my trails demands sharp focus on my feet, without which I'd surely trip or fall. In some places a fall would be very bad. But inside of that focus, my mind and my heart are working things out. I let them.

I run in nature partly because in the woods, in the hills and mountains, by the seashore, I am most able to draw the creative abundance of the natural word into me. When I run, I am reminded that I am not separate from the landscape. I am simply another element of the land moving through myriad elements indistinguishable from one another.

Running awakens my passions, my desires, my vulnerabilities and my creativity. In meditation I touch the creative void that exists everywhere around us, and within us, at all times. But as with the Tai Chi – the swirling black and white symbol taken to represent yin and yang – in the black there is white, and the white there is black: in stillness motion, and in motion stillness.

In meditation, my breathing (and my occasional physical reactions to the really hard and sometimes dark places I stumble upon) is the movement. In running, in particular on long, challenging runs, I inevitably find a place of quiet: I am not a man running in nature, but nature finding a still point within the motion.

And then, without a doubt, that stillness slips away, and is replaced by burning muscles and panting lungs as the winding trail goes on and on. On this particular day, I am awestruck by the sheer magnificence of the coastal landscape. I keep exclaiming to J that "I can't believe I live here!" It's pure delight to pass through this place, with these friends, and this life.

We finish our run on the beach at the end of Pike Road and rest in the sun, on a log, watching the waves pound the islets offshore. Then another short run out to Pike Road, and we reach the car after two-and-a-half hours on the trail and begin the drive back into Victoria.

Every step is a step into the unknown. Every moment is an opportunity to touch both stillness and motion. I will spend my life running toward stillness, and then, when I've finally reached it, simply keep running.

THE 29TH DAY

Today is Day 28. I looked at the calendar tonight and saw that it had been four weeks since I challenged myself to live in the present moment for one moon. That night I had lost, for the second time in just a few months, the same woman. I'd dropped Jenn at the airport and we'd said goodbye and then she was gone, and I had no idea when, or even if, I'd see her again. That's the way it's been for us. We live in different provinces, and have very different lives. We've both left long-term relationships in the last year, and we're not certain how to make a new one work right now. On top of that, I'm still struggling with the pain that I have caused in other people's lives; in particular, Kat's. While I know that she has forgiven me, I haven't forgiven myself. I returned home from the airport, dazed, and went for a walk around Fernwood, and dared myself to stay focused in the present. A fat full moon sat low on the horizon, and I figured if I could do this, alone, for one moon, then I might be able to just keep going.

"What pattern is this teaching you about?" I hear my friend Dan's voice in my head. That my challenge is to stay. My challenge is to stick it out. Leaving would be easier. By no means easy; just easier. Giving up on this relationship would mean some short-term pain, but it would pass in time, and I could move on. There would be scar tissue. Some things simply don't heal anymore. But in a month, or two, or maybe three, I could move on. That's my pattern. When the going gets tough, I walk away. I'm choosing to stay this time.

What are your patterns teaching you? That I fear fear itself. Fear closes my heart. Fear is the opposite of love. Fear kills love. I dread the cold hand of fear on my chest, on my throat. When I feel it taking its grip, I do anything I can not to give into it. But I am learning to invite fear in. Instead of running from fear, I am learning to "sit through" its icy wash.

Patterns: that I like quick fixes. One morning, I received an email that released the cavalcade of fear through me. Before I had finished reading the note, I was reaching for the phone, making things worse. The thought of sitting all day with the intensely uncomfortable emotions and uncertainty that the note provoked, was unbearable. But my haste to try and fix the problem only made it worse. Lao Tzu advises restraint as one of the three pillars of the *Tao Te Ching*. Step back, he says. Wait. Sit through it.

More patterns: uncertainty and vulnerability are also my nemeses, and yet I seem to attract them into my life. I run a consulting business; I'm a writer; I have fallen in love with a woman, knowing full well things would be tough. So what are these patterns teaching me? I've been trying hard to ground my happiness in what I think of myself, rather than what outside forces create for me. My attempts at staying completely centered in my own spirit have led me to a new form of self-flagellation. I'm in the middle of one of the most emotionally challenging situations of my life, and I'm beating myself up because I can't stay detached from its ebbs and flows! One day I'm up in the clouds, prattling on about bliss, and the next I'm crawling through the mud, browbeating myself for allowing external elements to jerk me around. I've got to go easy on myself.

"The object of your practice should first of all be yourself," says Zen Buddhist teacher Thich Nhat Hanh in *True Love*. "Your love for the other, your ability to love another person, depends on your ability to love yourself."

I still don't really think that I deserve to be loved. Sit through that too.

Tonight my two-year-old, Silas, learned how to say "love." He's felt it since the moment of his birth, I'm certain. He *is* love. He is made of love. But tonight as we wrestled on the couch, and I told him over and over again that I loved him, he repeated it, and then wouldn't stop saying it. He would throw his meaty arms around my neck and kiss me and say, "I luv you Dada." And then he would try it out on his big brother, Rio. And then say "Luv you Momma. Luv you An[d]y." He's learned that it's addictive to love.

I've learned a lot about joy, and about sorrow, in the last twenty-eight days. "The deeper that sorrow carves into your being, the more joy you can contain," says Kahlil Gibran. I'm nearly done with the whole carving bit.

I've learned that I can be pretty selfish. I get caught up in my own pain, and forget to consider that someone else is in pain too. It blinds me. It feeds my insecurity.

I've learned that I can try to run from all these things – sorrow, pain, vulnerability, fear – but they are always there with me. I can run, and fast, and hard, especially when I'm not loving myself as much as I deserve, especially when I want to feel physical pain rather than emotional or spiritual pain. Then I can run for hours, and let the ache in my body, and the numbing flood of endorphins, mask the ache in my heart – but it's always there the next morning.

I've learned that I can, in fact, sit through it. And I've learned that if I run *toward* love, and not *from* fear, I can run even farther. And that it doesn't hurt nearly as much.

It's been twenty-eight days. One moon. I am still in love. And sometimes it is bliss. And sometimes it is joy. And often it's very hard, and I don't do as well as I wish I would when facing my fear, my vulnerability and the impenetrable frustration or uncertainty. But I'm learning to be gentle with others, and with myself. And I'm learning what true love is.

One moon, come and gone. Tomorrow is the 29th day.

STEPPING INTO FEAR

For a short spell last winter, I studied Aikido again. It had been some time since I'd practiced the martial art, the last time being when I was in college. Then, my teacher was a brown-belt who had come to Aikido from a life of juvenile delinquency and street fighting. My teacher last winter was a black-belt who taught us to work with our own energy, and the energy of an opponent, to ensure that nobody in a conflict got hurt. One of the most powerful lessons that I took from that experience was to step into, not away from, an attack.

To step into, not away from, fear.

While studying Tai Kwon Do, again some years ago now, I was taught many defensive moves to fend off flying hands and feet. Step back, block, step back, block, block, counter-strike. Each movement was away from the attacker, until we were in position to land a punch or kick. Now, I was being taught to get in close to the attacker. Step into it, so that you can direct where the attack goes.

The practical application of this lesson in self-defence is as it pertains to my response to fear. My first instinct is to run from fear, to make myself so busy I don't have to face it. Drink tea, shave, shower. Fold laundry. Do the dishes. Focus on writing and on work. Do push-ups and chin-ups and tidy up the boys' room. But fear follows me, no matter how many times I step back and try to block, block, and counter-strike.

Now I'm learning to step into it. I sit. It's hard. Sometimes when I meditate and allow the emotion, the feelings, the pain or the fear to simply rise and fall, I am jarred from my silence and begin to stand. Where am I going to go, I ask, that I won't have to face you?

Instead I take a deep breath and invite my fear in. I say to myself, "Sit through this. Sit through this." It helps. Not always as much as I would like, but it always helps. Fear is just an emotion. It's just a response to something that I'm not yet able to face head-on.

For me, fear is almost always about some story that I've made up to explain what I don't know about my life. I don't know what is happening, so I create a story, and get attached to it. Stepping into fear, so I can get close enough to it and direct where its energy – its power over me – is going, helps me to overcome it.

NEEDLES

I hated needles as a kid. I understand that when I received one of my early immunizations it took several nurses to hold me still, and even then they had to pin me between a desk and my mother to make the jab. Years of allergy shots helped, but to this day I'm not wild about getting pricked.

So it seems paradoxical that I should seek out acupuncture as a means of healing. Years ago, when I was suffering from an inguinal hernia, my naturopath suggested acupuncture, and after several sessions the hernia stopped bothering me. A badly pinched sciatic nerve (a Lego-building injury: too long crouched on the floor with my nephew, building a giant spaceship) and more recently strained muscles around a popped rib, all made well again by a few needles.

For years I've been running on an injured knee. While visiting the B Bar Ranch in Montana, I was jumping a mountain creek, and in mid-air I saw that the rock I was about to land on was covered in a thin film of ice. I came down lightly on the ball of my right foot, but the momentum was too great: my leg shot out behind me, and my full body-weight came down on my left knee. I was able to walk back to the ranch, but for weeks afterwards I limped. Tai Chi helped, but I'm pretty sure I cracked something. I wear a brace when I run, and realize that if I want to do this for another thirty years, I'm going to have to take care of myself.

I used the knee as an excuse to visit a new Chinese doctor last night.

It wasn't really my knee that I wanted her to look at. It was my heart.

I met with Chantelle Zhuang at the Copper Mountain Clinic on Chatham Street in Victoria. We did the full assessment; all the questions about my own medical and emotional history. Yup, separation. That's right, lots of intense change. Kat's new man moving in, little Silas calling him "Dadda Andy" (which I think is pretty sweet, but it's a little painful too), the house I'm renting being sold, and of course, the end of a brief, intense love affair.

Family history? My mother's father died of a heart attack in his forties. My dad's dad had a non-fatal attack in his fifties and died of cancer. Mom has her challenges: alcohol in the bloodstream and a history of depression in the family. Dad is healthy, works to keep his weight down. Yes, Mom drank when I was in the womb. I tell Chantelle about my anger. How it manifests through my body. I tell her about my fevers, about the hives I used to get as a child. How my guts turn to mush when I'm in acute stress.

She flips through her notes: liver. The alcohol in the womb is linked to fire, she says. The liver controls emotions.

She asks me what I am feeling. I hesitate. We both say it at the same time: fear. "I've never felt so vulnerable in all my life," I tell her. The first tears trickle down my face.

She tucks the blanket in around my chest, and puts her hand on my heart. "You are safe," she says.

I don't remember the last time I felt truly safe. For the most part, I live my life outside the safety zone. It's my choice. I can't remember anybody ever telling me that I was safe.

The first four needles go in with their buzzing warmth, and I can feel the tears again. I'm so tired of tears that I fight them. She invites them. "Don't hold any of your emotions back," she says, her hand on my arm. I let go.

She puts in another thirty needles – in my forehead, my neck, my arms, hands, up my sternum and in my belly, down my legs, in my ankles, my feet and my toes. I can feel the energy pulsing. Tears flowing.

Chantelle sweeps the tears aside, dabbing at them as they pool in my ears. I am suddenly calm. Music. She slips from the room. Heat. I can feel the heat lamp on my chest, my belly.

I am fading into silence. I have to let go, without giving up. There is nothing in our lives to prepare us for such a bewildering paradox. But life is paradox. You either hold on, or you let go. Most of my life I've held on, held on, with a death grip, and then finally, in a spasm of defeat and relief, just let go. Given up.

Disappear. The music evaporates. The room fades. I dissolve into nothing at all. I am gone for some time.

"You have to be strong," I hear Chantelle at my side. I come back from stillness. I can feel the meridians in my body coursing with chi, with life, with love. Strong for what? To sit with uncertainty? Again? For how much longer? To be open to vulnerability?

It's twenty-four hours before the answer comes. To be selfless. To not leave. Work, love, family. To hold things together. To keep my promises. I am reminded of Barry Lopez's book *Desert Notes*: "I see that you are already tired. But you must stay. This is the pain of it all. You can't keep leaving." I will not leave. And I won't be pushed away. We're going to figure things out.

What I must do is let go of my own fear, my insecurity, and be strong and courageous and give what is needed – unconditional love – in order to break the cycle of uncertainty and vulnerability.

PHILOSOPHER KINGS AT THE ROYAL ROADS CAFE

I meet Dan at the Royal Roads Cafe. We shake hands and he asks, "How are you?" and I only smile and instead ask him how he's doing.

"Tired," he says, and I know he's not complaining. He's not the type. It's just a statement. "I've been getting up at 4 a.m. a lot lately. There's been a lot of energy flowing." We're not big on small talk.

Sitting down, I order tea and lunch and then ask him about the energy. He says that while he doesn't like to talk about it this sort of thing too much, he thinks that we're moving through an energy portal.

He must notice my eyebrows shoot up, because he quickly adds that it's not about all the astrological Sagittarius-in-the-fifth-house kind of malarkey (my word) but more about how energy moves through the universe, and that from time to time it becomes much more intense. Dan says that his personal take is that during these times it can feel very difficult to understand why things are so hard. His belief is that it's because we're literally being squeezed through a very small space – energetically – in order to emerge on the other side.

I'm laughing while he explains this. "Does this sound

familiar?" he asks. I nod, still laughing, but feeling an uncomfortable lump forming in my throat.

He's not one to quote the Bible all that often, he adds, but "it's like the eye of the needle. You can't take anything but your own soul with you when you pass through."

"So how *do* you finally move through it?" I want to know. If there's an express lane through the eye, then I want to jump on.

"You have to surrender," he says.

"Great," I mutter, "more fucking surrender." Dan explains that we must move from "f'ing surrender, to eloquent surrender." My read is that eloquent surrender is when you relax into the process of letting go, of stepping back, giving up control over outcomes. This is as opposed to simply saying, "I've had enough of this shit. I give up."

Our lunch comes and we begin to eat. I can see the question in his face: So how am I?

I tell him: Angry. Really angry. Frustrated. Confused. Vulnerable. Sorrowful. And sick and tired of it. He knows without having to ask, of course. We've been having lunch together once or twice a month for a year and a half. But even if this were the first time we'd sat down together, he would know. I'm an open book, and Dan is a highly skilled reader.

I say, "I was thinking about this meeting this morning, and I just couldn't believe that we were going to talk about my heart again. I'm sick of it. Work is going great, and while I sometimes feel fear and pain around my temporary parting from my children, this is what's got me completely, totally stuck. I just don't know what to do."

"We get together to work energetically," he says, smiling. "I am here to do is help you with the flow of energy in your life. To help you get unstuck."

When I tell people that Dan is my business coach, which he is, I quickly add that we don't sit around and talk about marketing strategies and new client acquisition. We talk about how the world really works: the flow of energy. And we both agree that energy is really just love that has yet to manifest in the world.

I explain to Dan that my greatest fear, the thing that gives me more pain than almost anything else, is uncertainty, the unknown. I know that every moment is a step into the unknown. But this morning, when I woke actually writhing in pain from a wine- and melatonin-induced sleep, this was a very new experience for me, too large a leap into mystery. I knew that something had to change. I just don't know what, or how.

He feels my frustration. I can tell he actually *feels* it. He challenges me: "Step into that frustration." I smirk. "No, really, step into it. Feel it. Right now."

I allow myself to actually feel what it is I'm feeling, rather than just rush past it. Some of the barriers I've been erecting start to crumble.

"More," he says.

I strip away a layer of protection. This is what he means by stepping into fear. My throat constricts.

"More," he gently pulls me.

I slip further into the sorrow. I can feel my eyes getting wet, and I back off.

"Step back into it," he urges.

I let the layers of protection slip a little more. I feel heat in my chest; my throat is tight and my face flushed.

"Now ask yourself, what pattern is this teaching you about?"

I let that question sit a moment, the sound of the room distant.

"Okay," he says.

I pick up my water and drink, but not because I'm thirsty. I'm just not interested in having a complete breakdown in the middle of the lunch rush.

"I didn't hear any voices telling me what the patterns were," I explain.

"When you feel that frustration, that pain, ask that question."

The lunch crowd is starting to thin out. "Why am I feeling this way?" I ask him. "Why are things so damn hard? And don't tell me about the damn portal."

"You tell me." Old coaching trick.

I sit with the question for a moment. A word came to me this morning during a pre-dawn walk. "It's penance," I tell him. It's a funny choice of words for a non-Catholic. I believe that I have to pay my karmic debt by telling this story, so as to wash myself of the mistakes I've made in the past. But penance?

"Because you've been a bad boy?" he smiles. I nod. I can't speak. "What do you need to do to take care of yourself right now?" he asks.

The conversation swirls around answers to that question while the waitress clears the table. Run. Meditate. But I can't expect it all to sort itself out at once.

We order dessert. Pie is good self-care practice.

I remind him of my attempts to apply the concept of self-referral over object-referral in my life. "I find that I am getting angry with myself that I can't detach from what is undoubtedly the hardest emotional situation that I've ever been in."

He laughs. "You're discovering new, sophisticated levels of self-loathing," he says, still smiling. "That's not the purpose of practicing self-referral."

We talk about the emptiness that is sure to come when I step into the unknown space that is before me. "Remember" he says, "the void was misnamed. It may seem empty, but it's where all true creation happens."

I share that I recently watched the movie *Peaceful Warrior*, which is based on the book *Way of the Peaceful Warrior*, by Dan Millman. When I first read that book, twenty years ago, I loved it, and I credit it in part with my transformation from a skinny kid who couldn't run to the street corner, to a skinny man who can run for hours up hills and along rough coastal or mountain trails.

The final scene in the movie is beautiful: Millman, a gymnast, is on the rings competing for the first time after a terrible accident, and he can hear his mentor Socrates's voice asking questions in his head, which Millman answers:

> What time is it?
> *Now.*
> Where are you?
> *Right here.*
> Who are you?
> *This moment.*

* * *

By the time our lunch ends, the sun has come out from behind heavy clouds. Dan and I part ways in the parking lot. I need to imprint our time together on my body, and I know of no better way to do that than running through the hills. The afternoon is warm, and I pad softly up the Lewis J. Clark trail to the summit of a ridge above the lake, mulling what Dan and I discussed, and my rocky path forward.

I'm going to need to be *This Moment* to make it through. I'm going to need to be kind to myself, to be loving with myself and with my boys and with Jenn, in order to find the peace we all desire. I run slowly, easily, amid the giant Douglas firs and down toward the lake, striding into my sorrow, my fear, my frustration, holding unconditional love in my heart, asking it all to reveal its patterns so I can squeeze through the eye of a needle.

RACING WAVES

The first cross-country race I ever participated in was a three-kilometre run, when I was in grade three or four. I was nine, maybe ten years old. I remember training for the race several days a week that fall, the sun just up, the crisp Northern Ontario mornings biting into lungs and legs as a handful of classmates and I plodded through Jack-pine forests and across frozen wetlands. Some mornings in the shower after those runs, our legs bled where blades of grass like razors had left their mark. I finished in the middle of the pack in that race, both on my team and in the whole event.

The next race I competed in was this past June. Time lapse: twenty-seven years, give or take. It was the Mount Doug GutBuster. A hot June day, with the race on my home turf, a hill I've run over at least five hundred times since moving to Victoria a few years ago. At eleven kilometres, with three ascents and descents of the bulbous dome, it was a grind, and the heat left me sapped. I came in 69th of 120 runners. Middle of the pack again.

I can't say that the Mount Doug race was fun while I was running it. It was hard. I passed out that afternoon while my two sons bounced on top of me.

Over the weekend, the Gunner Shaw Classic cross-country race was held at Thetis Lake, just outside of Victoria. It's another favourite place of mine to run, with winding trails that zig-zag up oak-dotted hills and down through dark, lichen-strewn woods. The Gunner Shaw has a reputation as being a bit of a tough race, with a rather unnecessary, but interesting, splash through a thigh-deep swamp at its midpoint. This plunge, in early November, provides the added bonus of turning the legs into blocks of frozen granite.

The final dash to the finish is across the foreshore of the Thetis Lake beach, which starts out nearly crotch-deep in frigid water. Some sprint to the finish. Several people take a dive.

I finished in the middle of the pack – 205th of 460 – running the nine-kilometre race in forty-five minutes. My best friend, J, reminded me that the Gunner Shaw attracts a pretty tough field: there were several Olympic athletes in the race. It was won in just over thirty minutes.

I was grumpy all afternoon, failing, I think, to properly rehydrate and replenish the system afterwards. Instead I jumped right back into single parenting.

My grouchy state was also because I didn't feel I ran as well as I might have. I felt drained of energy before I even got started!

While running, I kept pulling myself back to the here and the now, repeating over and over: "Where am I? *Right here.* What time is it? *Right now.* What am I? *This moment.*" But inevitably, as the weariness crept in, my mind drifted.

I forgot that I was running in a favourite place. I forgot that when I get tired while running I try to pull energy in from the rocks, the trees and the water. Instead I just tried to concentrate on being nice to people. I'm really not much of a competitor: when I hear someone coming up behind me (often) I make sure they have room to pass, and tell them they're doing great as they go by.

The day after the race, the boys and I ventured out to Fisgard Lighthouse National Historic Site. Only a few minutes from Victoria, and we'd never been. Silas is obsessed with lighthouses these days, though I don't know that he's ever seen anything larger than a navigation buoy. Fisgard was the first lighthouse built on Canada's west coast, and was operational until the mid-1950s. It's on the same site as Fort Rodd Hill National Historic Site, which served as part of the defensive system for the Esquimalt naval base up until World War Two. It's a pretty cool place for two little boys and their dad to spend an afternoon.

We visited the lighthouse, and I think Silas was pretty impressed. All Rio wanted to do was go to the beach, which is hard for me to argue with, so we did.

Silas collected shells and Rio raced back and forth along the shore. His running was so completely free. He would stand on a log along the tide line, and as the small waves washed over the gravel, he would launch himself along the beach, jumping and laughing as he always does when we are at the seashore. This is one of the things I love most about these dear, beautiful children, and there are many, many things I love.

When Rio stopped to catch his breath, I asked him what he was doing. "Racing waves," he replied matter-of-factly.

"What for?"

"It's for my exercises," he said.

"Is it fun?" He simply nodded. "Do you ever win?" I asked.

"I always win," he said, his pants wet to his knees, his boots sloshing with salt water. And off he ran again.

I can't wait until Rio and Silas and I run together through the woods. And we won't be racing the clock, or each other, but simply racing for life, racing the trees that blur past, racing the waves, racing the spinning Earth. At East Sooke Park we've run along the sandy foreshore for hours, jumping logs and dodging boulders and getting our feet soaked and laughing like fools. It's the purest expression of running I know. It's freedom incarnate. It's joy. It's bliss.

We took a break from running to have a snack. Rio found a rock and brought it to my attention. I had asked the boys to find something beautiful that we could bring to Jenn, whom I love deeply and profoundly, and who will arrive in Victoria in a few short days so we can try again. We always try to find something beautiful for her when she isn't here. Beach glass, heart-shaped stones, something lost overboard far out to sea. This day it was a lovely russet rock with green stripes. We took a picture of ourselves with it to email to her, and give her the rock when she arrives.

What *I* found that was beautiful on that beach that day was a reminder of why *I* run. I've only recently enjoyed (the aftermath of) competitions. For much of the last few years, running has simply been the way I dissolve myself into the splendour of nature; to feel with my body the reality that I am nothing more than nature moving through itself. To let my heart and head have some time to do their work without my constant intrusions; to let my body do what comes most naturally – be completely free.

FAITH

"Faith is like a bird that feels dawn breaking, but sings while it is still dark."

— Kahlil Gibran, *The Prophet*

Somehow I just believed. Somehow, despite months of darkness, I knew that there was light. *We* knew that there was light. Three months have passed since I counted the days of the lunar cycle after saying goodbye. Now, Jenn and I are trying once more. What else is worth trying so hard for if not love?

Early moments in our relationship: lying on the sand at Botanical Beach, the heat of July soaking us, the pockets of water that teem with life stretched out toward the rippled horizon. Then we're exploring: she is showing me the secret world of tide pools, places I might otherwise walk past with merely a glance. It's not the life beneath the water that I marvel at, but the life dancing in her eyes. That's the moment I fell in love. *That very moment.*

It was like falling into one of those tide pools. A shock. Unexpected. This wasn't supposed to happen. But there was no struggling against it.

Early moments: the dizzy delirium of falling. The way

she looks at me. When she smiles it is like the sun coming out.

In those early moments I saw a lifetime of possibility. This is how I want to feel for the rest of my life. It was that light, that possibility that helped us navigate very troubled waters. The darkest moments before the dawn.

We needed time to sort out our own troubles and put the past behind us. She asked me to believe in her. To trust her. It became my mantra. I would meditate on those words: I trust you; I believe in you. I believed in us. I had felt dawn breaking.

During the darkness I held on to that belief. That trust. I had been prepared to let go, forever, if that is what was needed for her to be at peace. Her peace was what I dreamed of, and was prepared to give her, even if it meant goodbye once and for all. But when she walked through my door, I knew that my faith, my belief, my trust in us had been vindicated. She knew too.

Faith is a bird….

Mornings in her arms. We slip down the Oregon Coast. Become enchanted by sea otter play. Have normal nights. Dream together. Watch salmon spawn. It was easy. It was the hardest thing I've ever done. But it was easy to have faith. Despite the darkest of times, the fear, the vulnerability, it was easy to have faith.

We're not out of the woods yet. There will be many dawns when we must hold our faith before morning finally comes for good. Maybe morning never really lasts, but like the diurnal rhythm everyone shares, we simply pass through mornings and nights over and over, believing, trusting, and falling more deeply in love.

HEARTS AND HOPE

I am in Hamilton, Ontario, at the Hamilton General ICU. My stepmother, Mabel, was admitted to the hospital after suffering chest pains this week. Two days here is enough to provide some order to a man's priorities, and teach an important lesson about the true nature of life's barriers. In September Mabel had a heart attack, but made a seemingly speedy recovery. But over the weekend she experienced chest pain, and managed to take some nitroglycerin before she and my father went to Joseph Brant hospital in Burlington, Ontario. Tests showed that she had significant blockages in the arteries leading from her heart. Bypass surgery was scheduled for Thursday. On Wednesday I flew from Victoria to be with them.

Hamilton General is a sprawling complex in a down-trodden neighborhood of the Steel City. But it's home to a top-notch cardiovascular surgical facility, and staffed with the region's best doctors and nurses. While Mabel entered the surgical theatre, my father, Mabel's children Pat and Alice, my sister Chantal, and a family friend sat in a room called "The Heart Investigation Unit and Operating Waiting Room." We made small talk to keep the fear at bay.

Mabel's surgery was successful – quadruple bypass – and by evening my father and Alice were able to see her. Friday, and we're back in the hospital for the day, visiting with Mabel, and sitting in the cafeteria, watching the snow fall. Today it's just my father and I. After a while we return to the ICU, mostly for a change of scene. Everybody in this room is here because someone they love is undergoing heart surgery. I look around the room: people sit in little groups and talk quietly. One man sits alone contemplating the pale wall across from his weary eyes. A woman next to me reassures her son via cell phone that her husband – his father – will be fine, after five heart attacks and his scheduled quadruple bypass surgery. I can feel the hope and fear thick in the room.

Fear that the failings of the human body, the choices we've made during our lives, and the genetic programming we've inherited have finally caught up with us, and with our kin.

Hope that tomorrow we'll wake up and those we love will still be by our side.

Last night I went to bed at my father's home exhausted, though I'd done nothing more than walk up and down the stairs to the cafeteria to find caffeine throughout the day. I lay in bed thinking about the people I love most: my father, my sister and my mother. My beautiful boys. My angel, Jenn.

It was the kind of day at the end of which I wished I could curl up with my lover and feel the warmth of her next to me. We speak in the evening and I can feel her so close, even though she is halfway across the country, in

Alberta's Bow Valley. I wonder what the hell I'm doing wasting even a single day not by her side? And where are my children? I'm thirty-seven years old and I still struggle nearly every month to pay the bills. What am I doing messing around like this?

I lay awake for a long time, my mind rearranging everything from my parenting style to my living arrangements; my career path to my living room furniture. The barriers that keep me from reaping the effortless state of inseparability with my family, my work and my love seem trivial when I'm lying in bed, thinking of the faces of families in the ICU, wondering if their husbands, wives, fathers and mothers will be at their sides in the morning.

SANCTUARY

Another sleepless night. Another day at Hamilton General. By midday I'm feeling overwhelmed by the pain of the place. Mabel is making an extraordinary recovery. How can someone have open heart surgery on Thursday, and on Saturday be so full of life, of love? Of faith? I walk down the now familiar halls, feeling the press of sorrow in some of the hospital's palliative spaces, amazed at the resilience of this amazing woman. We survive the most extraordinary things.

By the end of the afternoon my nerves are shot. Too much sorrow. Too much sadness. I seek shelter and find the multi-faith chapel on the hospital's main floor. It's peaceful there, with no comings and goings.

I've been walking around for hours waiting for release. I let go. Tears, of course, though I swore there would never be another. I curse myself at first, and then give up and let go again. I slip into meditation and try to remember my vows. Patience. Peace. Love.

When I slip out of the stillness, I realize I'm famished and head to the cafeteria to eat. At a table nearby I see a man I've noticed for the last few days, who I've said hello to, but not stopped to talk with. I've been absorbed with my father, with Mabel and with my own self-pity.

His name is John. I invite myself to sit with him while

he eats dinner, drinks tea. We chat. A week ago he fell while drawing a bath, and for half an hour was trapped as scalding water doused his face, head, neck, shoulders and chest, and he shouted for mercy. First, second and third degree burns scar his body. He has no hair left. He's ashamed of his own face. "The morphine was great," he said. He doesn't remember how he got from Kitchener to Hamilton. "I just woke up and I was here." He has five kids. "Have you had any visitors?" I try to be tactful. "It's been a hard year," he explains. "I didn't want them to see me like this again." As we say goodbye, I take his hand and hold it for a while.

Nobody should go through this alone.

John.

Diane, who I met yesterday, whose husband, emerging from his fifth heart attack, asked for a divorce because her business was losing money. She had slept in a chair in the ICU waiting room for two days while he underwent bypass surgery.

Sanctuary: a place of safety.

Sometimes it seems that everything about our existence on this spinning Earth is precarious. Sometimes it seems that love itself is the only thing that makes us safe.

PRAISE

It's the last day of my impromptu visit to Southern Ontario, and I'm ready to head home. These have been cold, dull, gunmetal days. The sky yet hangs in tattered rags; light snow fell overnight. My father invites me to church. He is a believer. I am too, but not in God, or Jesus, or the Holy Ghost, at least not in the way that he is. He knows this, but wanted me to come to church to witness first-hand something that is so important in his and Mabel's life. It was a decade ago now that he informed me that he and Mabel had been born again. I think it was a pre-emptive move on his part to keep me from launching into one of my regular tirades about organized religion.

We enter the hall and people greet my father and ask about Mabel. A man at the door shakes my hand, welcoming me. We move toward the sanctuary, and my father receives hugs and handshakes, and there are offers of food and other assistance. Finally we are seated, toward the front, where he and Mabel always sit.

This isn't the church that I attended on Christmas Eve and Easter as a child. Instead of an organ, there's a youth-led rock band. Instead of a cloak, Pastor Brian wears Dockers and a golf shirt. Instead of symbolism and ritual erected as a barrier, there is a down-to-earth belief that you can speak directly to God through your heart.

The service starts, and the band launches into a couple of rock and roll spirituals, including a vaulting version of "Amazing Grace." They lyrics are projected via PowerPoint for all to sing along. Hands and voices are raised. Indeed, I can feel the power of the music, and I tap my feet as I might at a concert. And why not? Music is one of the shortest routes we can take to connect with the miraculous. And maybe that is just another word for God.

When the band takes a break, I lean over and tell my father that if they had played music like that in church when I was a kid, I might have gone more often.

Next the children are hustled from the sanctuary downstairs to where they will attend Sunday School. My only memory of this ritual was attending a few classes where we did a lot of colouring. They had the big 64-packs of Crayola crayons – the ones with the built-in sharpener – which was all right by me. I don't remember anybody talking with me about God or Jesus there, although I might not have been paying attention (why would Sunday School be any different for me than, say, regular school?). Or maybe we were colouring pictures of Jesus?

I recall that over breakfast that morning my stepsister's son Ian talked with his mother about various passages from the Bible. I think he might have quoted some scripture. He's six.

Rio, who is also six, can quote Scooby-Doo. He's an expert at finding crabs under rocks. And he can sing most of the lyrics to several Jim Cuddy songs. We all have our own predilections.

After a few announcements, there are prayers for members of the congregation. I like the way these folks pray. It's conversational. There's none of the Latin chanting that I recall from my early experiences in the Catholic Church. It's just, "God, we're asking that you look after Mabel and Bob," and so on.

I can feel the power of the words, and of the congregation's loving intent, on my father, and I can sense him feeling alone, his wife still in the hospital and absent from his side at church maybe for the first time. I take his hand and hold it tightly while Pastor Brian finishes his prayer.

Do I believe in the power of prayer to heal? Damn right I do. Prayer focuses our intent, and with that we are able to direct the energy of the universe. I believe the energy that combines to create matter is susceptible to the energy released through the power of our intention. Loving intention is the most powerful of all, because love is pure energy, and when directed toward another person's well-being, it can create miracles.

When the congregation of the Burlington Alliance Church prays for Mabel's swift recovery, hundreds of people's loving, heartfelt energy is directed toward her. Yes, it has been proven that prayer makes a difference.

So does meditation. The universe responds. I'm not the one to explain how, or why, and I don't need anybody to provide the overly simplified explanation that "God responded."

Our prayers and meditation are a means by which we consciously influence how the building blocks of the universe — energy and information — are assembled. If so, then our "prayers" call "God" to organize energy into matter in a way that heals. Enough loving hearts willing someone to be well evokes a powerful response in the quantum field, which again, might be just another way of saying "God."

Believing in the power of meditation to reorganize energy and matter is no stranger than believing that an omnipotent being has control over how someone's heart responds to quadruple bypass surgery.

While the congregation prays, I meditate. I focus my heart on Mabel and envision her well, her own heart whole and beating. I focus my heart on my children, so beautiful and so far away. And I focus my heart on Jenn, also so beautiful, and also so very far away. I aspire that my meditation should be pure love, for that is what prayer could be. Selfless, pure, unconditional love. I'm trying.

It occurs to me as the service ends why people gather this way each week, aside from the question of faith. Simply put, it feels good. The room is alive with the energy of so many good people thinking so many kind, loving thoughts. It is alive with music. It is alive with what

Christians might call the movement of the Holy Ghost, and what I call bliss.

It is in the act of giving praise that we connect with something so much greater than ourselves, so much more vast and beautiful and lovely. If we have to call this "God" and accept His word without question in order to see ourselves as part of something miraculous, fine. But that's not my way. I don't need the answer handed to me so neatly packaged, all the questions answered without any room for doubt. The universe is far more complex, and far stranger, than the notion of an unseen creator controlling all human destiny.

But praise is what connects us – all of us. We might all praise creation, in its myriad forms, and its myriad explanations, as the life-giving, love-sustaining force on the earth and throughout the skies. In that praise – be it in church, in meditation, song, dance, physical and spiritual love, art, or communion with nature – we can find harmony with the essential fabric of the universe.

TRAIL NOTES: PART TWO

What are you not being truthful with yourself about?

What illusions are you holding on to?

What fear are you stepping away from? What
would happen if you stepped into it?

When you feel pain or frustration, ask,
"What pattern is this teaching me?"

Who can you bring peace to right now
with a simple smile or hello?

If you knew you were going to die, what
would you do differently?

You are: why aren't you doing it?

PART THREE
Over Rolling Country

The steep precipices on the outset of the run have levelled off to more gentle, rolling country, but there are still hills to climb.

Victoria, BC, remains home base, but Jenn and I are spending a great deal of time travelling back and forth between the coast and her home in the Bow Valley. The constant motion is unsettling to both of us. I find myself constantly missing someone.

I continue to write, and my second book, *The Cardinal Divide*, is published. *The Darkening Archipelago*, the next book in the Cole Blackwater mystery series, is planned for the following year. I get a job at the Royal Roads University Foundation.

In the heart of winter, at a place called Morning Glory Lakes in Yoho National Park, I ask Jenn to marry me.

A THOUSAND
NORMAL THINGS

The moon crests above Grotto Mountain. The air in the Bow Valley is crisp: I haven't felt this kind of air in my lungs for a few years. In the morning I run the trails along the benchlands above the town of Canmore. I've come to visit Jenn in Canmore to put my anxiety about this place behind me. It's been eight months – I thought forever – since the night I drove here over the Continental Divide to drop her off, and every day we are growing closer.

Catching up with the world after a few days in hibernation, I look at Asha Hope's blog. My friend and colleague Will Horter, and his partner Claudia Campbell had a little baby girl on Thursday, born fifteen weeks premature and weighing less than eight hundred grams. The next few months will be a daily trial for little Hope and her lovely parents. Looking at the photos on of Hope in her sealed incubator, I can't help but imagine how much Claudia and Will must long to hold her. With my lover's arms around me, I close my eyes and say a prayer for her.

Then I check in with the Facebook page of friends Joel Solomon and Shivon Robinsong. On Wednesday of last week, Shivon gave Joel one of her kidneys (in a hospital, with doctors looking on) as his were slowly shutting down, the result of a lifelong disease that has finally caught up with him. Both are well, buoyed by an out-pouring of love, as Shivon's kidney now does its cleaning thing inside Joel.

Out of habit, after visiting Asha Hope's blog and Joel and Shivon's Facebook page, I clicked on the *Globe and Mail* site, and as I was doing so I caught myself thinking: "I wonder if there will be any news about Asha?" Then I shook my head at how asinine a thought that was. There is nothing really important in the news. There is never any report on the thousand normal things that make up each and every one of our days and nights: hope and despair, joy and sorrow. The magic of life, the ecstasy and wonder of every single moment.

The sun sets behind Mount Rundle. The sky is indigo, except where stars prick the tapestry of dusk. It's just another day. Another thousand normal, extraordinary, heart-wrenchingly beautiful things.

PULSE

I'm sitting on the stairs at Victoria Gymnastics, watching Rio fly through the air, his sandy blond hair streaming out behind him as he launches himself off a mini-tramp. He's getting good at this, pushing himself in a way that leaves me awestruck. Between the mini-tramp and the tumble track, he dances on a mat to a rhythm only he can hear. Watching him physically grow up is such a precious gift.

A few hours ago I was flying (though not through the air, thank goodness) myself, running up and over the hills of Thetis Lake. There is a rhythm to this too, and a pulse. Once, when my best friend, J, and I were running up the steepest ridge on Mount Doug, we checked our pulses after making the dash from bottom to top in twelve minutes: 190 beats per second. While not quite the pulse of a hummingbird, which can beat 1,200 times per minute during flight, it still felt awfully quick.

Sitting on the stairs, watching Rio, I become aware that I'm swaying forwards and back. Forwards and back. It is my pulse that is moving me. Sometimes if I sit with one leg crossed over the other at the knee, the top leg actually bounces. Today the rhythm of my heart is actually moving me back and forth. I'm hoping that such a prominent pulse isn't a bad thing.

Forwards and back. The pulse. The heart pumps because of electrical waves generated by the sino-atrial node, a section of cellular tissue that is located in the right atrium of the heart and acts as the body's natural pacemaker, creating a "sinus rhythm" (not to be confused with the metrical blowing of one's nose when suffering from allergies).

The sino-atrial tissue is composed of special cells called cardiac myocytes, which generate the electrical pulse. In essence, the heart is a muscle that generates its own electrical cadence, which causes the contraction and expansion of its cells and results in the pulse of blood through our bodies. Anybody who isn't awestruck by that simply isn't spending enough time marvelling at the miracle of human life.

These waves of electricity pass through us and out of us. We can measure them with electrodes attached to the skin. Researchers have shown that these electrical waves extend far beyond the body. As tools for measuring this human electrical rhythm become more sophisticated, we are learning that the field encompassed by a human pulse seems almost without practical limit.

If someone were to sit down next to me on the stairs at the Victoria Gymnastics club, they would be sitting down inside the electrical field of my pulse. They would be sitting down, in a sense, inside a part of me, and I them.

We are a little naive to think that who we are is

encompassed by the seemingly solid demarcation of our epidermis. We breathe in, and we take in the world around us; it mixes with blood pumped from our hearts; and in a quick wink, it is circulated to every cell in our body. And just as quickly, the byproducts of our existence at that cellular level are circulated back, deposited via our bloodstream into our lungs, and then we breathe out. We are released back into the world around us. Forward and back.

But of course, even that thick layer of skin that keeps everything – bones, lungs, bladder – from dropping onto the trail as I lumber up the rocky hills on the Saanich Peninsula: even that is almost entirely not there. And so I am a pulse of electricity, moving among other pulses, exchanging both matter and energy with everything and everyone I meet. That's both really nice-sounding and a little creepy.

Over the weekend, I think about pulse. On Thursday night I swim with my children, marvel again at Rio as he twists and turns underwater, and at Silas, his wrestler-like arms wrapped around my neck as we bob along with the current in the whirlpool.

Friday is gym. Friday night, Jenn, back again from the Bow Valley, and I go to a farewell party for a friend and colleague and walk home in the dark arm-in-arm. Saturday we take the boys to Whiffen Spit, near Sooke, where Rio can dance along with the waves, and Silas hunkers down to get intimate with a stick (it's a paintbrush, he says) and the earth (his palette).

Sunday we head to Clover Point. Fly a kite. Play soccer. Throw a Frisbee. See fire trucks and a new fire boat. Race along the rocks on the beach. Drink hot chocolate at the end of the day.

It's a perfect weekend, and by the end of it, I'm more deeply in love with all three of these people than I ever dreamed possible. We're caught in each other's pulse. It's the most amazing place to be.

RUNNING TOWARD THE SUN

It's the first sunny day of the month of February. Every part of me yearns to be on a trail, running beneath the sun. There is a push and pull to the winter months. Short, grey, rainy days pull me toward lethargy. My body wants sugar, carbs and a couch. But I know that to endure a west coast winter, I must push myself out the door, even if my mind and body protest, to keep running. And on any sunny day, the imperative is even stronger. Drop what you're doing, and grab your shoes.

Mount Doug is my destination, and I plod up the familiar trails. Last month Jenn and I travelled to the Baja. It was a good trip, and it strengthened our connection. I managed to run a few times through the desert, pounding along ridges and hills, shredding my shins, knees and thighs on cactus and thorny shrubs until it looked as if I'd been in a knife fight with a two-foot-tall assailant, and had lost.

But I drank too much beer, and our diet seemed to include a pound of pulverized avocado every day. When we returned we both got sick, and then I was travelling with my consulting business, which kept me off the trails for another couple of weeks.

But this morning there are no excuses, and so I tramp along the path, slanting rays of sun warming my face, and coaxing me onward. It occurs to me that I've spent more than my share of time this winter mired in melancholia. More than just this winter, really. This last year. I'm supposed to be searching for bliss, I recall, and yet I keep finding blah. The cycles of my life continue to repeat, and time and time again I find myself trudging toward these summits with a tear-stained face. People say to break the cycles, but I don't think I want to. Instead of breaking them, I'll bend them, angle them upward. As this trail I'm on winds between Garry oaks and out over a rocky bulge, I push the angle of my cycles toward the sun.

Work, family, love: it all comes down to this: every single day is an opportunity to make rich the experience of our precious time in this fragile and fleeting life.

My body now loose, my head clear, my back warmed by the morning's dazzling light, I push over the summit and back down into the woods again. It's okay to be in the darkness now and then. I know the way. My body intuits rocks, roots, hidden obstacles. What I know for certain is this: my life now and forever is infused with the most extraordinary love I could imagine. I am deeply and profoundly grateful. The love given to me is the greatest gift of life's myriad offerings.

I will not get in the way of this. I will relax into this ecstasy, this bliss of being loved. I will put away fear, doubt, guilt. I will run forward, upward, toward harmony.

I will run toward the sun.

MORNING GLORY

Light snow falls and cloaks the trees. They look like phantoms, their forms stark against the dark shadow of the mountains beyond. It's early spring on the coast, but still the deep of winter along the Continental Divide of Yoho National Park, when Jenn and I ski up the fire road toward Lake O'Hara. The crisp air tightens our faces and turns our noses red.

Ours is not an alpine start – far from it. It's 4 p.m. before we begin, and after 6 when we reach the lake. Above, the fabled ramparts of Wiwaxy Peak jut like limestone gendarmes into the milky sky. It's dusk when we reach the Elizabeth Parker Hut. Perched on the edge of a snow-hummocked meadow, the hut is backed against the dark, protective shapes of Odaray Mountain and Mount Schaffer.

Jenn beams. This is her element. Winter, snow, mountains. To see her so happy is my heart's delight. We are most in love when we're out of doors, high in the mountains, on the ocean, in the hills. Jenn has a depth of knowledge of these landscapes and seashores that leaves me breathless. To see her tilt her head toward the sky and laugh at the snow is pure magic.

It's been ten years since I stayed at this rustic hut in these marvelous mountains. A fire is warming the century-old logs when we enter, people I know from my past life in Canmore are up for the night with two young kids. We stow our gear in the smaller cabin, light a fire and heat the place up as we prepare dinner and curl up on the benches, reading, drinking wine from a box and chatting with old friends. We sleep deeply, peacefully, curled in each other's arms.

The morning is grey, but not the kind of grey we get on the coast. Mountains stand in dark contrast to the mottled sky, their faces shadowed but comforting against the gently falling snow. Jenn's enthusiasm and her love of these ranges is contagious. I didn't believe, when I moved from the Rockies three years ago, that I would miss winter. But it's hard to not fall back in love with a season that brings such delight to the woman you want to spend the rest of your life with.

We ski through the woods, watch lichen sway in the breeze like summer dresses; see the tracks of rabbit, tracks of squirrel, and here, a set of tracks that merge with our trail. Bobcat? More likely lynx. We ski along beside the tracks for a while, charmed by the living forest around us.

Then down a long slope and into an open meadow beneath the implacable face of Cathedral Mountain. Flat places on the otherwise undulating landscape tell us where the Morning Glory Lakes are, far beneath the snow.

Jenn drops to the ground and makes a snow angel.

The wind pushes us down the valley, but we stop again

amid the soft, naked forms of Lyall's larch. There is a moment amid the snow and mountains and the Morning Glory Lakes where all my life seems to fold into a singular burst of joy and light.

I've been carrying around a set of rings – one was my grandmother's and the other my mother's – for the last few months, waiting for the right moment to do this. Now I fear dropping them into the six feet of snow beneath us and having to wait until spring to find them.

I ask Jenn to marry me and, beaming, she says yes.

We ski down the creek and cross the lynx tracks again. We have a late lunch in the hut, and by 4 p.m. are skiing back down the fire road, faster now as we glide down the valley. Fairer now that our souls are entwined.

BIG AS THE SKY

Together Jenn and I pick up Silas from daycare, and then we drive straight to the airport, and within an hour, Silas and I are back in the car, now without Jenn. I spend a week a month in Canmore with her, and she spends a week or ten days with me in our lopsided Fernwood home; the rest of the month we are alone in our respective abodes.

Silas and I pick up Rio from after-school care and head home, and I'm in the door and cooking dinner before it dawns on me how many different lives I'm living. The boys have a bath, and I fold laundry, and soon we're clearing the table and making Rio's lunch for tomorrow. Jenn calls from the airport shuttle and asks for phone numbers for taxis in Canmore.

The boys and I watch an episode of the animated series *Avatar*, and we snuggle on the couch, and Silas, in his casual way, tells me, "You're a great dad, Steph," the way you might say, "You're a great fruit, Banana."

Recently Rio repeated the refrain from the song he wrote for me at the Calgary Zoo: "I love you as big as the sky." Then he said, "That's really big, because the sky never ends, 'cause it goes on into outer space."

I tried to explain to Rio that space has no beginning and no end, fighting my own impulse to question what, exactly, is on the other side of the edge of the universe as it expands at the speed of light. I tell him that the universe bends back on itself to where it started, and then I get confused, and instead we ended up reading a Dr. Seuss book about how many apples a lion, a tiger and a leopard can balance on their heads while being chased by a bear with a broom. The answer is ten. But not for very long.

Sometimes I ask Rio if he knows how much I love him, and he just smiles and points his finger upward, but I always tell him anyway.

I call Jenn and she's home. Home. I'm home too. We're both home, but 954 kilometres apart. Not including the Strait of Georgia, so I guess it's pretty damn close to 1,000 kilometres.

In a couple of days, I'll be in Canmore too. Then we'll be apart again. And then … I get anxious just looking at my calendar these days. Blocks of time with and without the people I love. I've got them colour-coded. It helps. Not much, but a little.

Home. It's where the people I love as big as the sky are. And it's a good thing the sky is so big, because it's got to stretch a fair distance to cover those three people at any given moment in time.

TRAIL NOTES: PART THREE

What do you need to do to take care of yourself
right now? Why aren't you doing it?

What is the most extraordinary
ordinary thing in your life?

What amazes you about yourself?

What are you running away from?
What could you run toward?

PART FOUR

Striding Out

A shift occurs. The country is still rolling and there are still hills to climb, but they don't seem to cost as much. Our bodies respond to the landscape and our minds are no longer pocked with so many voices.

Meditation leads me further into an exploration of suffering and the path toward conquering it. After twenty years of study, I begin to identify more and more as a Buddhist.

Jenn and I travel to India.

We move her worldly possessions across the Continental Divide to Victoria and live together in Fernwood. All the while we have plans to return to Alberta. I realize it wasn't the place that inspired fear, but my own suffering.

My ephemeral position with Royal Roads University comes and goes, and through that passage I begin to discover my dharma.

Jenn and I are married.

NAMASTE

When Jenn and I first started discussing the notion of a trip to India, I was reluctant. My trepidation came from two principal concerns. First, we would be away from Rio and Silas for three weeks – a long time for me to go without seeing the boys. Second, India has a reputation for being a dirty, noisy, chaotic, illness-inducing country where it's hard to find a clean toilet. I didn't think I would handle either of these anxieties well, but when the opportunity presented itself to piggyback on the tail end of our friend Lisa Matthaus's year-long sojourn on the subcontinent, we jumped. I shelved my fretfulness: I would look at the three-week absence from the boys as an opportunity to step into my fear of being separated from them.

You see, so much has changed in our lives over the last year. When Jenn and I spent two weeks in Baja last January, I worried that Rio and Silas would forget me. It was the longest I'd been away from them, and it was painful. I worried that the guys would turn to their step-father, Andy – who is a great man – as their primary father-figure. I know this may sound ridiculous, but it was my fear nevertheless. Over the last year we have all grown so much as a mashed-up family that when I bid the boys goodbye the day before my departure for India,

I harboured no concern that they would forget or replace me.

On the matter of toilets: I stocked up on sanitary wipes and resolved not to worry about things I can't control.

India was everything I feared it would be, and so much more, and I loved every minute of it.

It was dirty beyond our wildest expectations. I was not prepared for the garbage. It's everywhere. Even in beautiful, natural places like the beach cliffs of Varkala, in southern Kerala, great cascades of garbage spill down the precipice and onto the beach. For the vast majority of the country there seems to be little in the way of garbage collection: you just jam your trash into a bin, box, under your house, in the open sewers, into the woods or over the nearest embankment and hope that the cows, which wander pretty much everywhere, eat it.

It was tremendously noisy. A din rises nearly constantly from every street, alley and laneway. The blaring of car horns is omnipresent. The rattle of every conceivable form of transportation vying for limited space fills every populated locale in the country with cacophony. The noise can be maddening, but there is also music there. India certainly has a soundtrack.

The country is greased with systematic chaos. India doesn't have rules. Okay, there must be rules, but they are so unlike anything that we follow in the West, and particularly in Canada, and most particularly in sleepy little Victoria, that there may as well not be rules. The pandemonium originates principally from the roadways, where traffic seems to operate in a free-for-all that if practiced in North America would, simply put, land every single driver on the road in jail. Forever. But that isn't the extent of it. There is a perfect disorder that at once makes you wonder how anything ever gets done, and leaves you scratching your head when it all does.

It was illness-inducing, but not nearly as bad as we had prepared for. Jenn and I brought a small pharmacy with us in our first-aid kit, prepared for just about any malady that might strike. I had an upset stomach – a persistent *gurgling* in the gut – most of the time I was in the country, but it wasn't really that bad. You could never, ever drink the water that comes out of any tap in that country, and salad or any vegetable that wasn't peeled was off my menu in all but the nicest hotels. But all in all, we fared well in this regard.

And I never had a hard time finding a clean toilet. The johns on the trains were a little dirty, but no more so than nearly every toilet I've visited in a bar on a Friday night, or any single outhouse in a campground in North America. In fact, in the airport in Mumbai on the way home, a man practically knocked me over and burst into the stall I was about to visit in order to personally clean the toilet seat for me. It was already polished to a high gloss. I felt like I had cheated him when I only took a leak. He was waiting to hand me a paper towel after I washed my hands. I felt like asking him to come home with us.

So India met all my stereotypical, prefabricated expectations and then just kept right on going.

What I was utterly unprepared for was how extraordinary the Indian people are. They are beautiful. Recall that this is a country with 1.2 billion people in it. At 3.2 million square kilometres, it is one-third the size of Canada. In Canada there are 3 people per square kilometre. In India, there are 375. You are never alone in India. The people are everywhere, and you would imagine that with so many folks stacked atop one another, they might be a little testy. Not so. You might also imagine, given that India suffers from terrible, bone-crushing poverty, that they might regard comparatively rich white tourists with scorn. Not so.

Often when walking down a street away from the tourist centres or through crowded markets blissfully void of white travellers, Jenn and I would be regarded with blank faces. It would be easy to misinterpret this as hostility, but instead it was curiosity. And my guess is that some travellers do, because so many eyeballs staring can be intimidating. But it is not unfriendliness; it's the gaze reserved for a rare sighting. And how did we choose to greet these onlookers? Smiles, waves, handshakes and the exchange of names and stories.

Early on we vowed to greet all these curious eyes with warmth and friendliness. Lisa told us that her secret to survival was to smile and laugh, to which I added "wave," and greet people with the familiar "Namaste."

It's the Sanskrit word that I wrote a little about in *Carry Tiger to Mountain*, my 2006 book on the *Tao Te Ching*. It means "the spirit in me greets the spirit in you." In the book, I joked that I was learning patience and compassion while waiting in long lines in banks and post offices by repeating this word. This word, and the meaning behind it, has helped me remember that everybody I meet is part of the tangled matrix of life across this humble planet.

In India I greeted damn near everybody with sincerity and Namaste, though I only occasionally added the hands pressed together as if in prayer. This all started with the immigration official at the airport in Mumbai when I arrived, and ended with the poorly organized and scattered security officials who gave me grief as I was leaving. And included everybody in between.

The fact that the people of a whole country traditionally greet one another that way – by honouring the spirit in one another – is an extraordinary thing. When we waved to people and smiled, they almost always smiled and waved back. Many wanted to know where we were from, and what our "good names" were. Many wanted to shake hands. Often I found myself in a small crowd of Indian men, telling stories and laughing with them, while they laughed with, and likely *at*, me. I enjoyed countless wonderful conversations, often in broken English, with countless wonderful people.

Near the end of our journey Jenn and I were in the port

city of Ernakulam. We had fled the touristy areas around Fort Kochi and taken a ferry across to the mainland and spent the day following our feet through crowded markets and bustling city streets and finally found ourselves in an upscale fabric store. From behind a towering pile of tablecloths, bedspreads, pillow cases and shirts, I greeted a fellow shopper – an Indian woman – with my usual Namaste, and she said, "Oh, you've learned our language!" I laughed and said, "No, just the one word."

But it seems that it's the right word. Two spirits greeting each other. One word, the right word, long-lasting smiles, laughter and a wave was what my too-short journey to India was all about. The right word, here, there, anywhere, now: Namaste. Spirits greeting one another.

THE ELECTRIC
CURRENT OF SPIRIT

It was the stars that taught me about the electric current of spirit in India, and inside us all.

Spirituality isn't something that happens on Sundays in India. It isn't confined to the church or the synagogue. It is a daily, if not hourly occurrence throughout the country. It is everyday life. Nearly every little town has a temple and temple tank, most have mosques, their loudspeakers announcing prayers five times a day.

Hindus account for about 82 percent of India's population, Islam roughly 12. About 2.5 percent of Indians are Christians. Sikhs account for another 2 percent, and less than 1 percent are Buddhists. The remaining point is made up of Jains, Parsis (followers of Zoroastrianism) and Jews (who at .0005 percent of the population still constitute over half a million, more than the 350,000 Jews in all of Canada).

But more than the formal religions and spiritual practices, which have often divided Indians along bloody and violent fault lines, we observed a powerful current of spirit that seemed to charge everything in the tiny corner of India we visited, and we could imagine it permeating the rest of the enormous country.

For me that electric current of spirit burst to the surface one evening in Varkala, near the very southern point of the subcontinent. Jenn and I were sitting atop the cliffs on the southern part of the town, looking out at the Arabian Sea as the sun slowly sank toward the horizon. It was still hot, and we had been out in the town all afternoon, and then swimming in the ocean, and were enjoying the peace at the close of the day. The sun, as is its custom, disappeared before actually meeting the horizon (pollution makes for such lovely sunsets), and as night overtook day, stars began to appear. We watched for an hour as darkness drew up all around us, the stars punctuating the deep blue above.

And then something amazing happened: the stars began to coagulate along the level horizon. We watched as more and more stars appeared on the ocean's verge, and as the darkness grew it became impossible to discern where the sky ended and the sea began. They were lights from fishing boats – thousands of them – and they spread across the Arabian Sea for as far as our eyes could see. It dawned on me that for each light we could see on the horizon, there were at least one or two men, and maybe many more, settling in for their supper, and then to sleep on the floors of their open boats; a simple awning or tarp all that would separate them from the vastness of heaven.

I've long gazed at the heavens and marvelled at our collective arrogance in believing that we are the only intelligent life in the universe. Maybe at this time we are,

and maybe we're the only supposedly intelligent life that struts about yammering on cell phones while fouling our own nests to the point that they are toxically uninhabitable. But it is pure hubris to think that among all the ancient and long-extinct stars we can see in the heavens, we are the only "life."

I squinted my eyes a moment, as I sometimes do when trying to perceive the world as it really is: a maze of energy and information swirling in clouds like dust. No hard edges; no beginnings and no end. Things became clearer. The single, ocean-like soul that spreads across this tiny orb called Earth reaches far beyond into the vastness of space.

We are all points of light in that soul; all unique and varied waves on that singular ocean. I pressed my eyes shut to better see: nothing separates us from one another except the dimness of our senses and the prejudice of our training. It's not a matter of needing education to see the world as it really is, as one; it's simply a matter of experiencing it.

The current of spirit that electrifies India charges us all. It's just that in India it is inescapable.

I took Jenn's hand in mine and watched the stars dance across the sea and the sky; the sun set on another enchanted day, the dawn just a few short hours away.

BUBBLES

One of the first things I did when I got back to Canada from India was go for a run.

Running wasn't really an option in India. I did bring my shoes and a pair of running shorts, but I didn't harbour any illusions that I would ever get to hit the trails there. It's just too hot, and I just couldn't see myself running with a big enough knife to cut the air in front of me.

After more than three weeks without any cardiovascular excursion, I was in need of run, so I drove to Mount Doug and did a languid lap around the outside of the hill. I walked a few of the steep bits and cantered down the rocky front side: I was just happy to be moving under my own power.

I was still in full-on India mode, smiling at everybody, waving, saying hello. I managed to check my impulse to say Namaste, but I certainly thought it a lot. What amazed me was how few times people actually said hello back, or returned my friendly grin. Several iPod-adorned runners didn't even hear me, and I'm pretty sure they didn't see me either.

I realized that in North America, we spend much of our time in bubbles. We create them around us, with our homes, fences, yards, security systems, vehicles – we need to have so much space around us all the time – and our iPods and our resolution not to make eye contact at any cost. There isn't enough space in India for everybody to have their own little bubble. You try to have your own bubble *there* and it gets burst pretty quickly.

It's not that there aren't places in North America where we're all packed tightly together. Many times, getting off the GO Train at Union Station in Toronto, I've been swept along in a tide of grumpy, myopic humanity pressing toward the stairwells and through the underground caverns of the station. People have actually done a double take when I hold the door open for them, or dare to comment on the kind of day it is.

It may be the sense of entitlement we seem to have here about space that creates our bubbles. We think we are entitled to a lot of space around us, and the privacy that it conveys. This is anathema to how Indians seem to carry on their day-to-day lives. It's not that they don't want privacy; it's just too much to expect in so crowded a country.

While exploring the Chor Bazaar, also called the Thieves' Market, in Mumbai, I was actually pinned for a few awkward moments in a crowd of people pushing between vendors' stalls and cattle while someone tried to drive a motorcycle through the tightly pressed space. It was very hot, and Jenn was well ahead of me, dealing with the gawking and sometimes inappropriate Muslim vendors and shoppers, and for a second I really didn't want to be where I was. I turned to assess my situation, and a man behind gently put his hand on my shoulder and guided me through the morass of human, bovine and mechanical stagnations. The moment passed and we continued down the bazaar. The hand on my shoulder said to me: this is just the way it is here, and we've all learned to get along so close to one another.

I think something else bursts the bubble: tolerance. There is a tolerance of one another, at least so far as caste and class and religious divisions allow. Indians tolerate one another in each other's space, lives and country. They don't regard other people as interruptions or annoyances in their lives, but rather as extensions of themselves.

And finally there is this: people seem genuinely happy. Despite having some of the worst poverty and some of the most dismal living conditions on earth, people seem generally joyful. This makes the bubble less necessary: when you're happy, it's okay to let others into your world.

I've spent a fair amount of time in a bubble, or trying to create one, or wishing I had one. I've spent pretty much all my adult life, and much of my adolescence, seeking out solitude and salvation in wild places, as far from other people as I am able to travel under my own power. I've not been the most tolerant of the presence of my fellow humans under the best of circumstances. Even before Jenn and I travelled to India, I was trying to be more understanding of other people when I passed them on the trail, on the street or when packed together on Vancouver's SkyTrain or a streetcar in Toronto. I genuinely like people, and want to connect with them. Smiling or saying hi or making small talk helps erode the myth of isolation that creates the pervasive loneliness so common across this continent.

In short, I'm trying to be tolerant, compassionate and happy. It's been a couple of weeks since our return from India, and I'm still trying to live outside of my bubble.

WAVES

Chest-deep in the Pacific Ocean, Jenn and I are encased like giant black caterpillars in thick wetsuits, clinging to powder-blue and pink surfboards. Above, the sun is shining, but here on earth the water, in early April, is frigid. Every now and again, water warmed by my body is joined by a trickle of ocean that seeps down my back or through my gloves, and I remember how cold winter really is.

We're novice surfers but already can taste the hint of perfection that comes when we are able to stand atop a wave and experience how the ocean feels as it moves across the skin of the earth. We catch a few more swells and ride them and get put through the ringer a few times, and while we're bobbing along in the ocean, Jenn says, "The last time we were in the ocean it was the Arabian Sea."

Then, the water was warm. We were in Varkala. We dove through the breaks and floated north in the current; the afternoon sun was so hot it was hard to be out in it. Varkala is a temple town. For more than two thousand years, Hindus have made a pilgrimage to Janardhana Temple; each morning and evening they descend the temple's steps and make their way down the crowded streets to the ocean, where they receive the puja blessing, and where many then wade into the ocean as part of their religious ritual.

I don't know the significance. I've read that in the sacred waters of the Arabian Sea, Hindus can plead for salvation for the souls of their departed loved ones. What is clear is that these waters *are* holy. Step into these waves, and you are stepping into healing waters of salvation. So are all the waters of this sacred earth.

The waves break against our bodies as we bob in the Pacific, clinging to our surfboards. In doing so, these waves carry away a little bit of us, cleanse us of what wounds us, what makes us afraid, what comes between us and that which we love. And these healing waters carry something *to* us as well; the buoyant peace born from the knowledge that all humankind are ripples on the sea of creation.

CONDUIT

This May marked the twenty-first year I have been writing. Of course, I had been stringing words together before that. In grade five I won an award for my writing: my first and only award to date. But May 1988 was when I began *consciously* writing. It was when I decided to *become* a writer.

My first writing venue was a street lamp near my suburban Burlington, Ontario, home. My first genre: really awful, angst-ridden teenage poetry. My first topic: heartache, loss, nature, the doors of perception (I was reading Jim Morrison's poems at the time) and love. Yes, the kind of love between two people, but also a bigger love that incorporated the rest of humankind, and the universe.

With the exception of Jim Morrison, not much has changed.

Then, as now, I felt that I was a conduit through which the universe might communicate. Not necessarily very well; nor have I ever thought I had singular domain over this. It's just that writing is the tool I have used to channel my particular part of the universe's energy.

For the longest time I believed it would be black and white photography. But working in a professional photographer's studio for a few months after graduating from high school pretty much killed that ambition. I still love to view the world through my camera, but it is when I am at the keyboard that I feel most in touch with the creative energy of the universe.

In 1994 I started seriously writing fiction. I penned my first short story while living at Grand Canyon National Park that winter. In 1999 I spent the better part of my summer researching and writing a novel called *Across the Universe*. I got about three hundred pages into the project and stalled. Summers were short in the Canadian Rockies.

In 2003 I began writing the Cole Blackwater mystery series. Writing can often be hard work, but writing about this hard-edged, soft-hearted environmental sleuth was easy. Once I established a pattern to my writing, the words just flowed. Making time to write, and to write every day, was a challenge, but once I was seated at the computer, following a storyline scribbled on a sheet of butcher paper or typed out in rough, the words poured out of me like water. It was as if, after many years of searching, I had found the tap and turned it on.

The Cardinal Divide took its own sweet time to congeal, but not so for the second and third books in this environmental murder-mystery trilogy.

Circumstances played a role in the ease of this writing, mind you. Because I found myself, in the early days of 2007, living on my own, with Rio and Silas at my home just three nights of the week, I began the practice of rising at 5 a.m. I would write for three uninterrupted hours each morning, and because my consulting work was steady but not overwhelming, I could return my attention to the misadventures of Cole Blackwater throughout the day to edit and revise what I had written that morning.

I wrote the first draft of the second book in the Cole Blackwater series in twenty-eight days.

The third book followed soon thereafter. It was much more intricate, with a very complex and disturbing antagonist, so it took two full months to pen the five-hundred-page first draft. Writing these books was pure bliss. It was easy. They flowed. I knew beyond a doubt that I had discovered my dharma. (Editing these books, especially the third book, *The Vanishing Track*, was a different story altogether.)

Dharma is a Sanskrit word that means purpose in life. According to Deepak Chopra – whose book *The Seven Spiritual Laws of Success* has meant so much to me over these last few years – there are three components to this ancient law.

The first is that each of us has a unique purpose in life. The universe has conspired to give us human form to discover that purpose. The second component of dharma is to express our purpose with our unique talent, or talents. The third component of dharma is to serve humanity, and all creation, through those talents.

If you can discover your purpose, express it with your unique talents and serve others doing this, then you might tap into the unlimited abundance that the universe is able to provide. This is not merely physical wealth, but emotional and spiritual abundance too. This is what I was referring to when I made Jenn, now my fiancée, dinner, and talked about the three simple things I wanted more of in my life.

By discovering my dharma – or what will certainly be a part of my life's purpose – I have been able to tap into an abundance I had never imaged existed before in the universe.

When I am writing, sometimes I "disappear." Stephen Legault, physical form – bald, slouched over the keyboard, cup of tea growing cold close at hand – dissolves. What remains is part of the electric current of spirit I have described elsewhere, in contact with everything else in the universe.

Momentarily I am a conduit through which the ideas can pass, through me, out my fingers, and onto an electronic page. It's an imperfect universe, and so the creation is also imperfect. The universe, obviously, could care less for spelling and grammar mistakes. It also struggles with past and future tense. It has an annoying tendency for repetition. But when I am truly connected with my dharma, my purpose, I am a pipeline through which the universe's energy passes, and I am left to experience the sensation of bliss.

As I noted in the first essay in this book, during my stint writing the third Cole Blackwater book, the experience was so overwhelming I had to stop writing altogether, press my hands flat against my desk and close my eyes to allow the sensation to move through me. The cold fire passed through my entire body, bringing tears to my eyes.

Anything that feels that good can't be too far off from what the universe intends for you.

You and I are temporary beings, having taken physical form, and we have a chance to experience our single, or many, unique reasons for being, if we choose. That purpose need not meet anyone else's notion of meaningful. Your purpose may serve humanity in ways only you might understand. But when we are living our lives in a way that expresses that unique purpose fully, there can be bliss so profound that it stops us cold. It is that bliss that I live my life for, and through.

RUNNING TOWARD RESPONSIBILITY

Up the side trail from Burlington's Walker's Line, I run through the second- and third-growth forest, over a tiny bridge that spans a seasonal creek. The rocks are covered in moss and the trees spaced far apart, giving these woods an airy, almost parkland feeling. Above this forest loom the limestone cliffs of the Niagara Escarpment. This is where I learned to hike, take photographs, camp and run. It's also where I learned an important lesson about responsibility.

I'm in Southern Ontario for work with Royal Roads University, and visiting my parents for the weekend. Whenever I'm here, I try to run on the trails I knew so well as a teenager. While I started running as a kid in the forests of Northern Ontario, and got more serious about it as a teenager trying to keep up with a track-and-field-star girlfriend, it was in these woods of beech, maple and pine that I first discovered what I was running toward, rather than away from.

The trail switchbacks through the rocks; it's the middle of summer and although it's early in the morning the temperature is already approaching thirty degrees. Wet with sweat, I peel off my shirt and hang it on a branch for later retrieval. Reaching the top of the steep switchbacks, I clamber up the last fifteen feet of limestone with the unwanted aid of a ladder.

When I first started exploring the Bruce Trail, there were no ladders here. In the 1980s my friends and I ventured to these trails to explore and hike, packing hot dogs and pop and spending our days traipsing along this route, discovering Mount Nemo's caves and limestone cliffs. The ladders, paid parking, pit toilets and fieldstone viewpoint are new, a testimony to the area's popularity. I am glad more people are enjoying this trail, but I bemoan the need for such improvements.

Once on top of the escarpment, I run north along the ridge. The rocky trail is challenging; the path traverses outcrops of fractured limestone that once formed the shore of Lake Ontario, and now jut like tiny ribs out of the earth. The woods whizz past in a dizzying whirl of greens: so many that I doubt they all have names. Cicadas, the insects whose wings buzz out the song of Southern Ontario's summer, welcome me back to these forests of my youth.

When I was growing up in nearby Burlington, I came here to run away. Once I had my driver's licence and my own camera, this is where I would come to escape what was an often unpleasant home life. My parents divorced when I was sixteen, and the years after that were troubling. I fought nearly constantly with my mother so whenever I could I fled to Mount Nemo and other locales along the escarpment to find peace. Here I shot black and white film, hiked with my friends and often just sat on the edge of the earth, alone, letting nature do what my home life could not: give me tranquility. As I grew more fit and steady on my feet I began to take my first trail runs.

Those runs aren't like the ones I do today. They were tentative and self-conscious; I wasn't an athlete when I was in high school. I mostly ran the streets around my home late at night so nobody would see me. But in the woods behind my Burlington townhouse – the forest that was was eventually cleared to make way for the 427 toll highway – or along the rocky escarpment of Mount Nemo, I could relax and be myself.

I was running from the challenge of being a teenager in a fractured home. I was doing something I would get very good at over the next twenty years: running away from taking responsibility for my own problems. I ran from my growing sense of anger, fear and frustration.

What I didn't understand at the time was that when you run away from something the trail is a loop. You finish running and find yourself right back where you were, mired in whatever it was you hoped to escape. What I learned during those tumultuous years after my parents' divorce was that blaming someone else for your suffering in life was easier than taking responsibility for it. If you blame someone else for what's wrong in your life, then you just keep circling around, finding temporary relief as you run in the other direction.

Sooner or later, the trail leads right back to the source of your suffering.

I pass the stone overlook, Toronto's skyline a fuzzy blur through the pollution and haze that hangs in the summer air, and say hello to a few people out for a hike on the Bruce Trail. Then I continue along to the rocky promenades I remember from my high school days.

I ask myself: am I still running away from things? This hot summer morning, I'm perfectly at ease running through these woods. It's been two decades since that difficult time. I've suffered through my own separation, and while my life is yet turbulent, I've at least learned to face my suffering and take responsibility for it. It's made it easier to rebuild a relationship with my mother: I no longer blame her as she has blamed others for her own suffering.

What I realize is that running toward something is far more productive than running away from anything. *"What am I running toward?"* I ask myself, my feet finding their footing as the trial descends along the crags. I'm running toward taking responsibility.

I own the problems in my life. Nobody else has created them for me: I alone am the author of my distress. I've made decisions over the course of my life that have led me to where I am now. Many of those were good decisions: I think of Rio and Silas and of my upcoming marriage to Jenn. Some of them were bad. But they've all brought me to the here and now, and simply deciding

Bad things happen; how each of us responds to challenges is a choice. That choice reflects our essential character and ultimately shapes whether we have a joyful life, or one mired with sorrow.

Down the trail, through the woods, over the mossy rocks: every footfall is a line under the fundamental truth that we choose who we are every day.

A CETACEAN MODEL
FOR PATTERNS

"This afternoon is about looking for patterns," I announce as Jenn and I walk down the trail to Botanical Beach, along the rocky terminus of the Juan de Fuca Trail. We're two hours' drive north of Victoria, but we feel like we're at the edge of the world.

The day is overcast; thick mats of fog roll over the strait that separates Vancouver Island from the mainland Coast Mountains of Washington State. Flat light: the horizon will be dull, but the details of plants and the lush coastal understorey will stand out in sharp relief; this is ideal for macro photography. It's perfect for close examination.

When I'm looking through the lens of my Nikon, more than just the details of my subject matter come into sharp focus. This last week I've become acutely aware of patterns in my life. We are creatures of habit, some say; I assert we are creatures of pattern. We're wired for patterns. Our brains like to follow them, making it easy for us to repeat, and hard for us to break, the patterns in our lives.

There are many scales to these patterns. Our bodies are made up of patterns of cells forming muscle, organs, skin, even our brains. Our brains themselves are complex machines composed both of physical and neurological patterns. Within them the electromagnetic pulse of thought and consciousness follows patterns and creates them. The vastly complex neural net that is both subject to and the creator of our habits, responses and reactions can sometimes seem a slave to the patterns of our lives.

Aware of the complexity of patterns around and within us, we sashay down the trail, zooming in tight to snap pictures of false lily of the valley and deer fern.

Zoom in even tighter, down to the cellular level, right to the foundation of our existence, and the patterns seem to disappear into random unpredictability. At this scale, where Newtonian physics is replaced with quantum mechanics, the expected patterns are lost. Electrons blink in and out of existence. Matter can exist in two places at once, and remain connected even if separated by vast distances. Electrons can even make the leap from one quantum state – or energy level – to another without passing through any state in between. This "quantum leap" is as close to instantaneous as is possible. Where the electron *goes* between quantum states is a mystery. The space and the time between one state and the other do not, for all practical purposes, exist. When an electron makes this leap, however, it creates photons, or light, and other forms of electromagnetic radiation, such as radio waves or ultraviolet radiation.

It takes something as indescribable as a quantum leap to make light.

We discovered some lovely designs on our short stroll to the surf, but as it turns out the patterns I was seeking weren't really the obvious ones along the leafy trail. I was looking for the reflection of universal patterns on the inner landscape, which must come as a big surprise to you by this point in the book.

Here we are forced to zoom out from the micro to the macro and witness patterns in our individual behaviour. Sometimes I think I am little more than a stimulus-and-response machine, so habitual am I in my response to events and thoughts. But even for the most habit-prone mind, it is possible to rewire the circuitry to create entirely new behaviour. Go wider still and witness the patterns between the organisms: society, civilization, humanity.

All this consideration of patterns at the micro and macro levels has a point. On the Thursday before our visit to Sombrio and Botanical Beach, my position at Royal Roads University, where for the last fourteen months I've been working at the Royal Roads University Foundation, was cut. Hard times led to a budget crunch, and my position, along with others, ended up on the chopping block. I was curious what would happen next, and what, if anything, this change meant.

I believe that the universe's pattern is composed, at the most rudimentary level, of random events. When seen at the microscopic level, the pattern seems arbitrary. It's only when we step back that the pattern makes sense.

I also believe that people can create their own patterns. When we interrupt our response to an event – an angry reaction, a comment made out of frustration, the clutching fear we sometimes feel – we are consciously remapping the neural network in our brains. We create new pathways. Part of the reason it's hard to change our behaviour is because the neural pathways in our brains are entrenched. They are comfortable: they like to keep firing along the same rutted path that they have always been firing along. My effort to interrupt my own anger over the last few years is case in point.

It takes effort to overwrite one pathway with another. In doing so, however, we might create new, healthier blueprints for our actions.

Finally, I believe that we can do this instantaneously, without passing through time or space between patterns. I am convinced that a moment of blissful insight can change how we perceive the world, and how we conduct our lives within it. Rare as they may be, these quantum leaps – however grand or humble – allow us to become part of a new pattern all together.

And when we do this we create light.

Jenn and I spent a few hours exploring the intertidal zone of Botanical Beach. The tide pools along this rocky shore are truly extraordinary, deep, festooned with sea grasses, teeming with life, rich with diversity and ripe with patterns. As we picked our way around the stone jetty that separates one beach from the next, we scanned the water offshore for signs of life, and found it. The telltale plume of mist and water rising high into the air alerted us to a whale just offshore. Jenn clicked away with the camera while I scanned and spotted for her. At first we believed we were watching a grey whale working its way along the bottom of the reef break a few hundred feet off the rocky coast, but a distinctive dorsal fin suggested otherwise.

The dorsal told us that a least one and maybe two orcas – the largest members of the dolphin family – were cruising along the rocky jetty. These "killer whales" were transients – not members of the local pods of orcas that these passages are famous for – and they were hunting. We watched for an hour or more. After the orcas seemed to vanish, the distinctive ribbed spine of a grey whale reappeared just a hundred feet offshore, this time in the thick mats of a bull kelp forest, a place where a baleen whale that feeds off krill really shouldn't be.

The experience was fascinating and thrilling, and left us curious. Jenn beamed as she watched the aquatic parade of creatures, and couldn't wait to get home to our shelves of marine guides to figure out exactly what we saw.

And I was left wondering about patterns. I started by searching for patterns at a very small scale – the forest floor – and ended up watching two members of the largest class of creatures on earth: cetaceans, commonly known as whales and dolphins. Jenn and I even joked that as we were crawling around on hands and knees, peering into tide pools, killer whales were chasing a grey whale a few hundred feet away.

We have to see all the patterns at once. We must tune ourselves to their overlap and their interplay. What is happening at the quantum scale in each and every one of our atoms is mirrored in the vastness of the dark green ocean below and the arching blue sky above. The light made by our leaps from one set of patterns to another reflects the perfect, if not mysterious, order of the in-finite and extraordinary universe. There is a meaning in these patterns. We can understand them. They can help us make the most of our brief, amazing lives.

MYSTICS ON THE BEACH

Rio, Silas and I reach the trailhead for Mystic Beach after 4 p.m. On our drive around the southern tip of Vancouver Island and up the west coast, we pass a forest fire burning north of Sooke, its smoke clouding the late spring sunshine. When we begin the short two-kilometre hike through the woods down to the beach, the smoke has started to tint the sky a deep burnt umber, giving everything a rich, rosy appearance. The world seems supernatural as we plod through the darkening forest.

It's an easy hike down to Mystic Beach, but Silas's five-year-old legs are still pretty short, and his pack – though filled mostly with light items of clothing, and the legendary Fred-e-bear – is bulky, so we take our time. That suits me just fine. My pack, containing the tent, our three sleeping bags, our Therm-a-Rests, food, cooking gear and two extra-large cans of Belgian beer, is bigger than most I've carried on week-long trips, so I'm happy to dawdle.

One of the great pleasures about hiking along the rugged western coast of Vancouver Island is the sense of anticipation that comes as we near the ocean itself. These woods are permeated by the influence of that great western sea; hike just a few miles inland and the forest is drier, less dense, and the tree species reflect their distance from the ocean. As we near the coast, the forest becomes darker, the trees more stalwart; the dells pool with water, and the understorey grows deeper and is cloaked in ferns.

Soon we hear the surf. Even though this stretch of beach is far enough south to be protected by the Olympic Peninsula across the Haro Strait, the waves still pound it, creating a rhythmic pulse that we can hear a kilometre away. That sound energizes us. The boys respond by picking up the pace. We three all feel the surge of energy that comes as we draw near the ocean.

I remember the first time I felt that electric energy. In 1993 a friend and I packed our bags and took the Greyhound to Vancouver. From there we boarded the ferry for the big island. It was my first trip across the Strait of Georgia. We hitched our way from Nanaimo to Tofino, and after buying veggies, wine, and fish fresh from the boats, we made our way to Schooner Cove. In those days you could still random camp there, and our intent was to meet some friends on the beach and then drive to the Clayoquout Sound logging protest camp the next morning.

I recall my pulse quickening as we descended through the rainforest and I heard the ocean for the first time, beyond the veil of trees. When we finally emerged through the tangle of shrubs on the foreshore, there was nothing to see. A dense bank of fog obscured the ocean – we could barely see a hundred feet up the coast. But we could hear it, and as I poked my way through the mist the ocean came crashing upon me. After we'd met up with our friends – how we found them in that miasma remains a mystery – we cooked our fish in a pit fire on the beach, drank the wine, and just before sundown the fog lifted and I got my first view of the majestic Pacific. It was worth the wait.

As the boys and I mount the fallen tree that has been chainsawed to create a hundred-foot-long set of stairs toward the beach, I remember the feeling of looking out over the Pacific for the first time. One night on the beach – the dome of heaven above; the thick, salty taste of the sea infusing tents and sleeping bags and wine, supper – and I was hooked. I dreamt about the ocean all that winter – while working at Grand Canyon National Park, no less – and those dreams brought my family and me to the coast many years later. And now those dreams have brought my boys and me to Mystic Beach.

The sun is low on the horizon as we finally clamber over the hedge of driftwood logs and drop our packs on the beach. The first thing the boys do is throw off their shoes and race down to the water. Silas, despite having been tired for the last few hundred yards, sprints for the surf. When he's a few feet from the crashing waves he begins "waterbending." He's a fan of *Avatar*, where a young monk named Ang is a waterbender – a skill that allows him to manipulate water to his will. Silas begins the rhythmic back-and-forth motions that remind me of Tai Chi. He is, of course, bending water; it's just the

H_2O in his own lithe little body that is being twisted and turned.

Rio races the length of the beach, up and down, skimming the margin of the sea, where the sand turns soft underfoot with so much salt water. As he bolts to the far south end of the beach he spots the waterfall that drops from the woods onto the sand, and soon both he and Silas are running back and forth through it. It's just a steady trickle, but it's enough that both children are soaked to the skin in minutes.

They do laps like this, running along the water's edge, the waves curling behind them, the mountains of the Olympic Coast blue on the horizon, and then dash through the waterfall, jumping and dancing in the spray.

This is what childhood should feel like. Their laughter is life's soundtrack.

Watching them run like this makes it easy to believe that no matter what happens in life, as long as you can keep running, laughing, jumping and dancing, everything will be all right.

I have to coax them away from the waterfall to help set up camp before the sun finally descends below the horizon. Sunset through the smoke paints the ocean, the beach and our faces red. We make a simple dinner of macaroni and cheese and I open a beer. Rio and Silas are famished, so I give them my portion, and when I'm doing the dishes at water's edge, Rio appears behind me, several spoonfuls of pasta still in his bowl, and he insists that I eat them. I promise myself that I will never forget this simple act of compassion from a son for his father.

For dessert we make popcorn on the stove and eat it while reading stories, resting our backs on a massive driftwood log.

Soon we pile into the two-man tent and listen to the wind in the trees above us and the ocean just a hundred feet away. The tent is getting too small for all three of us, so I sleep half-in, half-out, those same stars I once watched from Schooner Cove looking down on me now, so many years later. Silas clings to Fred-e-bear, the ragged, well-travelled stuffed bear that was mine when I was his age and has been passed from father to son.

Mystic Beach is named for its beauty, a nearly supernatural arrangement of surf, waterfall, sand and towering forest. But we're all mystics here. To be a mystic, some say, is to have special insight into the unknown, which is only revealed to the initiated.

For we three, sleeping in a too-small tent on the edge of the greatest ocean on earth, the insight seems simple enough: when you come to the place you have anticipated you should take off your shoes, run, dance and drench yourself in the dew of life. There is no better way to tell the earth, and one another, about your love for existence than to run barefoot across a beach at sundown.

To be among the initiated, you need only step away from the pavement, into the woods, the mountains, the desert, or onto the beach and be present to nature's quiet, persistent voice. Go as far as you are able; even if it's only a short way, you will find that the world, to the initiated, is filled with magic, every single minute of every single day.

UNION

We've all heard the expression that "we're all one." I've written about this myself many times, talking about my experiences with my children, and the mirror of nature that we all reflect. Two weeks ago Jenn and I were married. It was an amazing day, and the culmination of two years of days both wonderful and challenging, as two people in the early middle of their lives tied their worlds together.

We married at a small lodge in the mountains west of Canmore, Alberta, called Mount Engadine, and were joined by Rio and Silas, our immediate families, and a few close friends. The backdrop of the mountains, moose grazing in the meadows a few hundred feet from where we wed, and the circle of loved ones who joined us made our marriage magical.

I've long held that love is the most important thing in the world. I teach Rio and Silas that. I've not always been able to live as though love were paramount, but I've tried hard to demonstrate this belief with my actions.

On a sunny afternoon in the Rocky Mountains, I experienced once again the bliss that alerts me to my connection with everything else in the universe, and with the magnificent energy of love. I held hands with Jenn on the broad sundeck of the lodge before gathered friends and family and committed my life to her.

When Jenn walked out on her father's arm to greet Rio and Silas and I, who were standing hand in hand awaiting her appearance, I felt a tunnelling of my vision that I hadn't ever experienced before. I must have shooed the boys away to sit with their grandparents, because suddenly we were there, alone, facing one another. I was lost in her.

In that moment there had never been anything more beautiful in the universe to me than Jenn.

Carl Shields, our marriage official, read our service. It was simple and eloquent. We choose to include a passage from Kahlil Gibran's *The Prophet*:

> *Love has no other desire but to fulfill itself.*
> *But if you love and must have desires, let these be your desires:*
> *To melt and be like a running brook that sings its melody to the night.*
> *To know the pain of too much tenderness.*
> *To be wounded by your own understanding of love;*
> *And to bleed willingly and joyfully.*
> *To wake at dawn with a winged heart and give thanks for another day of loving;*
> *To rest at the noon hour and meditate love's ecstasy;*
> *To return home at eventide with gratitude;*
> *And then to sleep with a prayer for the beloved in your heart and a song of praise upon your lips.*

I fumbled the whole *I do* thing, thinking that Carl's

question was more properly answered (phonetically speaking) with *I will*, and then had to quickly add "I do" lest the whole service go off the rails (it's a present-, not a future-tense thing, Jenn reminded me later).

And then suddenly we were married. It's just a word; just a legal formality. But it isn't, really. It's an affirmation of one of the most profound aspects of the human condition. It's a celebration of what may well be the most unique experience of the fundamental backbone of the universe.

When I married Jenn, it was a public declaration that two human beings had come together in a union of the universe's pure energy, of pure love. And if time and the graces of that same universe are willing, it is only the very beginning of what we can do with that magnificent energy.

ONE MOMENT OF WILDNESS

There was a time in my life when I spent every spare moment in wildness. I was raised with wildness at my back. Beyond the mown expanse of weeds and the thousand-square-foot vegetable garden that was our back yard in Porcupine, Ontario, was a field of tangled shrubs and small trees bordered by an old double-track road; beyond that, a small creek sheltered by willows; beyond that, a single paper birch that stood on the edge of Mr. Mackey's field; and finally, the rough second-growth pine forest that defined my childhood and gave birth to my taste for nature.

These woods, and those that rambled away beyond the squared log home that my grandparents lived in for more than forty years on the Palmour Mine property, were the geography of my childhood.

Singular moments: cross-country skiing on the trails that my grandfather Lucien cut through the woods behind his home, and coming to the place where, like a miracle, cookies would materialize from the worn pack he always carried; cookies no doubt hastily packed by my whirlwind of a grand-mère, Evelyn. I remember one particular day as if it were yesterday: it was just he and I – grand-père and grandson – and a gift of precious time that will never occur again.

Singular moments: hunting for grouse with my father behind our Porcupine home. My father was an expert marksman who won trophies for trap-shooting. To watch him stop, swing the Winchester shotgun to his shoulder and fire in one fluid motion was heart-stopping for a boy of seven or eight. There would be an explosion of leaves and small branches in the woods and then he would walk into the foliage and return with a partridge, its body perfectly intact but its head astonishingly absent. My father would then field dress the bird and put it in his pack while the acrid scent of gunpowder dispersed in the crisp autumn air.

Singular moments: during the summer of 1979, when we lived in Elliot Lake, Ontario building a fort in the well of a tree that had been toppled in a storm in a woodlot behind our house. My friends and I hollowed out the well and, using scrap lumber and garbage bags, built an igloo-like structure which we convinced our parents to let us sleep in one night. I was eight; just a little older than my eldest son Rio is today.

I lasted until sometime after midnight. Of all the phantasmal sights and sounds that haunted those woods, it was an ant that finally sent me indoors. We had an old eight-volt battery-powered light in our hut with us, and its beam was angled upward toward the ceiling. In the circle of light it cast, we watched, horrified, as a giant creature circled our hut again and again, its shadow pressed against the flimsy plastic fabric of our makeshift walls. As the creature roved around the circumference of our abode, we would each in turn cower as it drew close to our backs. It finally dawned on one of us that if we were seeing the shadow *inside* the hut, then the beast had to be *inside* too: which is when we noted the ant running in manic circles around the rim of the upturned flashlight.

Skiing with my grandfather, hunting and fishing with my dad, camping with my buddies in a plot of forest spared the saw and the subdivision, fishing, hiking, the annual Christmas-tree hunt in the back forty, walking with my sister to inspect robins' eggs in the trees beyond the big garden: these and a hundred other moments of wildness are what shaped me and created who I am today.

Which is why I find it so perplexing that I have moved so far from my connection to wildness. And why, when recently Jenn and I spent a long weekend in the Rockies, a single-day hike in a wild, out-of-the-way place made my heart ache for more.

There is a creek that snakes its way between Mount Andromache and an unnamed peak to join with the Bow River just south of Mosquito Creek in Banff National Park, Alberta. The creek's name is Noseeum: it's named for an animal the size of a dust mote with teeth like a sabre-toothed cat's. This was our destination one hot afternoon over the August long weekend: it's a place I've been twice before, and have wanted to share with Jenn since we became a couple.

I moved to the Rockies in 1992. After a single season working for the Ontario Ministry of Natural Resources as a student park naturalist at Murphy's Point Provincial Park, I got a dream job as a natural history interpreter in Lake Louise, in Banff. I knew nothing about the mountains, but over time learned just enough to stay alive and employed, in part because my lot was thrown in with veteran park staffers Jim Woods and Jack Loustaunau. For three or four summers I lived with Jim, Jack and a motley collection of other seasonal park staff in a dark, dank, dismal locale called Charleston Residence.

But we were rarely there. We spent our time outside, and it was that time that defines my experience in the Mountain Parks. We hiked. We hiked a lot. And in 1993, when Jim and Jack and I met J, we became a team.

But it was Jim Woods who provided my inaugural experience with the true wildness of Banff National Park. It was Jim who taught me how to pack for a trip, what to wear, how to read a topographic map and use a compass, and how to travel "off-trail." In short, it was Jim who taught me to take my adventuring in the parks beyond the carefully scripted descriptions in the guidebooks (most of which were written by friends, and which are invaluable) and into the vast regions of the parks seldom seen by people.

Jim took me up Noseeum Creek for the first time. It was early June of 1992; I'd been in the Rockies for five or six weeks, and Noseeum Creek and the high mountain passes beyond were to be my first off-trail adventure. Like the singular moments with my father and grandfather, this one is engrained in my recollection.

Jenn and I shoulder day packs and head up the south side of the creek. The afternoon is warm, and within minutes we're feeling the sun boring into us. We find the familiar cadence of walking and talking, and inside of an hour we're at the base of a steep cliff where waterfalls thunder out of a deep gorge and trip across ancient stone cast aside in the last ice age. From here we can see where Jim and I made our ascent of the limestone steps that lead to Noseeum Creek's headwaters: a narrow gulf that is strewn with boulders and provides a steep egress to a table-like plateau nearly two thousand feet above us.

Jenn and I take a more circuitous route, but one with fewer objective hazards (fancy mountaineer-talk for rocks that might fall on your head). After laying stepping stones in the mouth of the creek where it surges from its canyon, we jumped across and scrambled up the headwall. Another ten minutes and we reached the top of the first of many deceptive benches that eventually lead to a sparkling meltwater lake.

On that hot afternoon in August, my wife and I looked back at the long, sensuous ridge of Mount Andromache, and I retold her the story of when J and I climbed that peak. It was during the feverish summer of 1995, when he and I were bagging peaks before work and after work and on the weekends. In one frantic week we ascended five mountains and got turned back by a sixth. Mount Andromache was one of the five, and it was a lovely scramble on a perfect morning. I shake my head at the memory of a time when all I did was wake up at 4 a.m. and climb peaks with my best friend. It wasn't so long ago, really.

Jenn and I make our way through a steep, forested glade, crossing another creek below a tantalizing waterfall, its spray filling the air with a cool mist scented with the essence of a mountain wilderness: sun-warmed pines tinged with seared limestone. I've written this so often over the last twenty years that I fear that I'm plagiarizing my own words: moving water is what stirs me and awakens me the most in nature. Our bodies are almost entirely composed of water, so when I'm next to a cascading creek or river I find it nearly impossible to ignore my kinship with the blood of the earth.

Wallace Stegner said it best when he wrote in *The Sound of Mountain Water* that "[b]y such a river it is impossible to believe that one will ever be tired or old."

Upward again, urging our protesting legs to plod along a small rise, we surmount yet another bench of tilted limestone. Jenn lies down in the sun while I scout our route, wondering just where the hell this lake has gotten too since I was last here, more than a decade ago. I scramble up another fifty-foot-high step and spot the reclusive thing, and then see Jenn striding along below. Reunited, we make the final approach to the shimmering lake and find a place in the shade to cool off.

All around, the landscape is bare and devoid of vegetation. This is raw earth; not so long ago it was beneath the rapidly receding Molar Glacier or its kin. Unnamed peaks rise up all around, dip and fold, and are cut by rivulets of meltwater. A few snow patches cling to the mountain sides below the merciless sun. Above, another few kilometres' walking, is the saddle that Jim and I crossed, on our journey, into the next watershed.

I'm not normally one to take the plunge, but being a coastal boy these days, the opportunity to cool my heels, and the rest of me, in a mountain lake is rare, so I strip down and dive in. Jenn complains that she might have missed the event while taking pictures, so insists I do a repeat performance. I oblige, shouting and stammering as I cut the frigid waters.

When Jim and I reached the lake, we kept on walking, crossing that high col above the watery shores to reach the headwaters of the Molar Creek and South Molar Pass. From there we carried on, dropping down to the Molar meadows, traversing miles of hummocky terrain that taught me my first real lessons in off-trail travel – don't get frustrated – and finally connecting with the Mosquito Creek Trail. The last dozen kilometres of our walk were on that well-worn path. It was my first really big hike in the Rockies; counting couldn't number all those that followed.

In 1992 I was just discovering what it means to be alive, on this glorious earth, in a wild place untrammelled by people. Today, eighteen years after I first visited the headwaters of Noseeum Creek, I am remembering again all those vital lessons.

Though sore feet and aching legs might have obscured it at the time, my long day in the mountains with Jim Woods was one catalyzing moment of a profound relationship with the earth. What began with my forays into the spruce and pine forests and on the crystal lakes of Northern Ontario became a vocation for me during the summers of 1991 through 1996, when I hiked a thousand kilometres a year, many of them in an Ontario MNR, Parks Canada or US National Park Service volunteer uniform.

But more than that, being amid the wildness of Banff and the other Mountain National Parks became a portal through which my perception of the world changed, and my place in the world right along with it.

I didn't have the language for it at the time, but even then I was aware that through my exploration of the natural world I was delving into my spiritual connection to the universe beyond. Then I spoke of nature and the mountains, and later the canyons of Arizona and Utah, as my temples. And of course they still are.

Now, I can add to this. Simply put, when immersed in wild country I know that I am closer to the basic elements of creation than nearly anywhere else. In the canyons of Utah, the folded peaks of the Rocky Mountains, my childhood forests of the North, or on a wild beach at land's end, I might touch the raw fabric of existence.

Since childhood I have experienced moments of blissful connection with the earth and the sky while in wild places. Here the illusionary boundaries between me and the living earth, its myriad creatures and the universe beyond are less palpable. Here I can, for brief moments, experience the rock-solid earth as part of the quantum soup that we wade through, unseeing, most every day.

These are singular moments: not unlike the feeling of connection that comes from a moment shared between father and son, or grandfather and grandson, we are connected to this sacred earth in ways more holy and more profound than we have the senses to perceive.

Jenn and I return to the car. We drive into Lake Louise, and for nostalgia's sake, drink a cold beer and eat dinner at Bill Peyto's Cafe at the hostel. If we were to slip a Blue Rodeo CD into the stereo it would complete the reminiscence. We're both dirty and sunburnt and a little tired, but exuberant for having been in the mountains for a day. At no time do I feel a greater love for my wife than when we are in wild country together.

I remember now what propelled me up so many trails, over so many unmarked passes between wild valleys, to the summit of so many craggy peaks: immersion in the world around me. Immersion: It's what I've been missing, living apart from wild places. It's what my decisions over the last five years have cost me. And though I don't regret the outcome of those choices, I'm ready to invite more wild moments into my life again.

The moving-away-from is of course as natural as the desire to reunite. And now I have so much more to bring back into the wild that might help me see it as I really is. And so much less that gets in the way of that view. As Jenn and I eat dinner, we discuss our pending move back to Canmore and the Bow Valley, excited that there will be many days like this one for us and our boys. One moment of wildness can reveal all that there is to know about the real nature of this universe of mysteries. One moment of wildness is a window onto the vast, sparkling nature of the soul.

THREE BY SEVEN

It's hard to know the right thing to do when it comes to parenting. There's no manual. There are lots and lots of books filled with advice, but no actual operational guide. And that, of course, makes it pretty much the same as everything else in life.

Rio turned seven in January. He seemed to go from being a little boy to a little man almost overnight.

In the yogic tradition, our lives are segmented into seven-year periods of development that follow the progression of the seven chakras. The first, or base, chakra is about connecting to the earth and the material world; it's about stability. About getting our footing in life.

The second, or sacral, chakra is about sensuality, creativity, enthusiasm and exploration.

According to the yogic tradition, the seventh year is a period of transition and contemplation.

Rio is moving through such a transition now. It's beautiful, and challenging, to be a part of it. In the end, the best I can do is watch, hold his hand and love him as he deepens his experience of this extraordinary life.

Earlier in the spring, Rio and Silas, who is now almost four and still very much connecting with the earth and seeking stability, spent an afternoon at Clover Point, looking out at the Juan de Fuca Strait. I was frustrated because the afternoon wasn't going as I had envisioned. It was cold, and when we traipsed down to Mount Doug Beach half an hour earlier, it was in the shade and felt like winter. I complained bitterly. I turned the two children around and, still complaining, traipsed them back up to the car and made for the more dependable Clover Point. The sun was out, but so was the wind, and my mood, which was sour from a day of too much city and too many responsibilities, was as biting as the breeze.

We settled onto the beach, and after a few minutes of sun and stones and waves I was able to relax. Silas clambered around on the rocks while Rio contemplated me as we draped ourselves over a driftwood log.

"Dad," he said, and the rarity of his using the word rather than the more familiar "Stephie" surprised me. "Dad, is it hard being an adult?"

"Sometimes it is," I said without hesitation, and then exhaled loudly into the chilly air. "But most often we just make it hard."

I turned and looked at him, at his beautiful face. "We have expectations about how things are supposed to be, and when they aren't, we get frustrated or angry and make ourselves unhappy."

Attachment leads to suffering. "Do you know what expectations are?" I asked.

He nodded. "Things that we hope for," he said.

"That's right, things we want to happen. We have stories playing in our head all the time about how our lives are supposed to be. When the stories don't come true, we are unhappy. Adults have a lot of expectations, and life often doesn't turn out the way we want. It's not that it's always bad. It's often very good. It's just that we can never really know what's going to happen, so we have to let go of our stories. Does that make sense?"

He smiled and nodded. "Why do you ask?" I said.

"You once asked me if it's hard to be a boy," he said.

"And is it?"

"No. Not really."

I pulled him over the log and held him in my arms and we looked for beach glass and he told me all the things that he wanted to be when he grows up. It was agreed that he could be all of them and many, many more. We agreed that I could be all the things I wanted to be too, and many more that I hadn't considered yet.

Early summer now, and Rio and I are lying on his bed, reading books. The boys spend about forty percent of their time with Jenn and me; the rest of the time they are with their mom and stepdad, Andy. Both boys spend a lot of time talking about their lives at their other home when they are with their respective parents. I hear about Kat and Andy a lot, as I think they hear about Jenn and me a great deal too. Sometimes, however, I grow weary of the list of cool things that Kat and Andy do with the boys.

If I could hand-pick a stepfather for the boys, I'd pick Andy. He's smart, funny, loving, adventurous and practical. He teaches them a lot, and loves them deeply. But I get pretty jealous of the fact that he gets to see them more than I do, and sometimes when I get my four nights with the boys, I just want them to myself. So I said to Rio, "You know, you told me you like to have adult conversations, so I'm going to tell you something in an adult way. When you talk about Andy so much all the time, it makes me a little jealous. I wish that when you and I were together that we could just focus on us, and maybe not talk about Andy all the time."

Rio looked at me and said, "Well, Steph, it's just that I like Andy better. He's funny, and he wrestles with me more." It wasn't said to be mean; it was said matter-of-factly. It felt as if someone had punched me in the stomach. I lay back on the bed next to my son and looked at the ceiling. He read his books. People have said some pretty awful things to me, and about me, in my life, but nothing compared to this. I felt sick. I felt like I wanted to run away. I felt like weeping.

Suffering is caused by attachment. I am attached to my love for my sons and for my wife. You never expect to hear that one of them loves someone else more. Especially not your seven-year-old little man. I fully expect to hear both my children tell me they *hate* me. I just hoped I had until they were teenagers before that happened, and it would be because I had stopped them from drinking *all* my beer.

But hearing Rio tell me he liked Andy more brought

all my fear to the surface. I lay there and looked at the ceiling and wondered what to do. Get angry? Yell? Run away? Cry? I had to take all that emotion and turn it; I had to take that frustration and anger and most of all, my fear – that black, oppressive fear – and turn it into love.

Fear casts a shadow over love, but love can overcome fear.

So I rolled over and grappled with the lanky kid and said, "Andy wrestles more, does he? We'll see about that!" and I put the little bugger in a half-nelson and pinned him. Well, not really. But we did wrestle.

It was a momentary victory: conquering fear; conquering my habitual angry response to fear.

But my dread didn't abate. For the next two days I felt angry and upset. Finally, when she was sick of my over-reacting to everything, being cantankerous and mean, Jenn said to me: "Why don't we just deal with what this is *really* all about. It's about you and Rio."

We talked it out. A seven-year-old can't know how much a simple statement can hurt. He may not even mean it. As Jenn told me, "One day the monster loves broccoli and the next he hates it."

A couple of days later, when I was dropping the boys off with Kat, I mentioned the story and she laughed and said, "Yeah, I think they like Andy better than *me* most of the time too."

It's best not to take things too seriously.

Recently Rio, Silas and I were engaged in a familiar

autumn tradition: we visited Ross Bay Cemetery, along the waterfront in Victoria. The leaves there are great for jumping in, and the boys love to create huge piles and leap into them. Who doesn't? The cemetery was little more than an interesting setting for our activities until Rio asked about all the headstones and who was buried beneath them.

"Some people get burnt up!" Silas helpfully added to our conversation on burial.

Rio shot him an angry look and then cast his eyes down. Then he started to cry.

"What's the matter?"

He hooked his arms around me and cried into my chest.

"I don't want you to leave me," he said, sobbing.

"I'm not going to leave you," I said.

"I don't want you to get burned up. I don't want you to leave."

It's hard to know what to say. "I love you," I finally said. "I love you more than all the leaves in the world; I love you more than all the stars in the sky" I said, repeating our familiar refrain. I held him while his tears dried. "Everybody dies someday. We just have to love each other as much as we can while we're here together."

I suppose that was enough said, because we built another pile of leaves and jumped up and down in it.

The message of that moment isn't lost on me: love them while they are here. They *love you*, you fool. Love them and then let them go. You don't ever forget about them; there isn't a moment you don't love them more. You just have to let go.

When Rio was born I dubbed him my little Taoist master. At first he didn't know it, but slowly he's coming to understand his role as my teacher, just as I have a role in teaching him.

It's worth considering just exactly where, in terms of seven-year cycles, the father in this equation is at: at thirty-eight, I've just entered the sixth stage, or ajna chakra. It's also known in some circles as "the third eye." This seven-year phase of life is when we might shed off our illusions in time to integrate all the qualities of each chakra and experience true reality. It's not easy. There is no instruction manual. The lessons come hard sometimes, if they come at all. It would be far simpler to just ignore them and watch TV.

Three lessons by a seven-year-old. A boy, so early in life, grounding himself, finding his feet and exploring his world. A man, approaching the middle of the journey, but also exploring the true nature of the experience of being human.

POWER UP

The long climb from the bluffs that form a sandy escarpment above Mount Doug Beach to the summit of the hill is about six hundred feet in elevation gain. It's a spectacular trail that weaves its way between sea and sky amid a dense, light-speckled forest. In the winter it can be very wet, being on the windward side of this coastal hill, and the vegetation reflects the damper climate: massive Douglas fir trees jut out of the fern-cloaked forest; red cedar and spruce compete for the light. The trails can become brooks during heavy rains, and more than once I've found myself calf-deep, jumping up the steps of a track-turned-waterfall.

But in the middle of this drier-than-normal summer, it's parched and makes for easy running. It's a good thing too, because once again I have much in common with the banana slugs I labour to avoid as I plod along through the woods.

I come to the place on the trail – or, more accurately, a point in my run – where I always seem to slow down. It's inexplicable. I'm less than fifteen minutes into my run and I'm feeling tired. It's the hump; it's the wall. I look at my watch and allow for sixty seconds of walking, and then begin again. I pass one of my favourite trees – a Douglas fir that is broader than my six-foot wingspan. It always gives me a boost of energy to power up the steep hill that rises above this primordial giant. Before long I'm on the trail that circumnavigates the rocky hill near its midpoint, gliding over the undulating terrain.

The sun peaks out from behind high clouds and the woods are momentarily transformed into a living cathedral of light.

I take the cut-off that veers upward again, scrambling over the polished stone that leads out of the dark woods and into an arbutus-pocked ridge that will take me to the summit.

This is where I struggle.

I think that I've run over the summit of Mount Doug a thousand times now. I've lived in Victoria since the spring of 2005 – four years at this point in the narrative – and for big chunks of that time I've run at Mount Doug twice and sometimes three times a week. Every time I come here, I run over the summit at least once. I haven't been keeping track, but a thousand sounds about right. Despite that, it's still hard work.

This morning when I started out, I set my mind to run for an hour and to run from sea level to the summit twice. But now, two thirds of the way into my first lap up the hill, I'm feeling empty. I stop, chiding myself for my lacklustre effort. I eat an energy bar. That helps. Despite having been running for more than two decades, I often get the nutrition part of the exercise wrong and run out of steam. I need to work on that too.

The food helps, but I know something else is even more important to my running: mindfulness, and the awareness of no-self.

When I run I find that as hard as a trail might be, it's made all the more difficult by the insistent intrusions of my overactive mind. Serious athletes talk about the "chatter" or the "monkey mind" that they must confront during competitions. I have a friend who is preparing for an Ironman race this fall, and she tells me that during her gruelling 180-kilometre training rides the chatter can be almost deafening. The voices in our minds can tell us over and over again that we can't do this. So just stop. Stopping is easier than continuing. Stop riding, stop running, and the discomfort will stop too.

It's the same voices that I confront when I'm in the empty room of meditation.

On the meditation cushion and on the trail, there is no place to hide. There is no escape.

When I'm meditating and confront something dark lurking in the emptiness, my inclination is to dart. But when I'm physically running, my challenge is to find stillness within before grinding to an embarrassing halt halfway up a tough hill.

Pushing through the discomfort of the climb, I borrow a trick from my meditation practice to confront the ruckus in my mind. I acknowledge the voices, and rather than try to banish them, I make friends with them. "You are just voices. You have no power over me. You speak to me, but I can choose to accept what you are saying or not. I choose not to."

This mindfulness takes the wind out of the voices' sails.

I glide over the summit of the hill and begin down the front side. My aim is to run the long, main trail along the leeward side of the hill all the way down, and then turn around and make for the summit again along the sandy, Garry-oak-studded slopes.

The second element of mindfulness that matters to me is simply maintaining present moment awareness. I can acknowledge the clatter of voices in my head that pull at my legs and make my movement heavy; or I can choose to reject what those voices are saying. And I can shift my awareness to the marvellous experience of gliding through the ancient forests of this tiny island park. I seek out rough, rocky, root-strewn, boulder-clad trails with plenty of downed trees and stream crossings because when I run on them I *have* to pay attention. The voices don't get to have their say if my mind is engaged with the world around me.

Weaving my way back up the six hundred feet of elevation gain is hard, but not as hard as I thought it might be (and certainly not as hard as the voices told me it would be). Once again I let go of the concept of self.

No-self is one of the fundamental tenets of Buddhism, and probably one of the most difficult to grasp. Most of us have come to believe that there is an "I" inhabiting our body, and that this "I" has a soul that is singular and unique. But the harder one searches for the "I" in ourselves, the more likely we come to see that there is no self home to answer the call.

Gautama Buddha recognized this two thousand years ago. Today we can affirm with science what the Buddha discovered through many years of meditation: no-self is the recognition that we are simply the local manifestation of the stew of energy and information that gives rise to all life, to all matter. We are at once individual manifestations, and at the same time seamlessly a part of all the rest of creation.

This is very helpful when we're addressing our suffering. Attachment to the notion of the self can lead to some pretty big hurdles to freedom from suffering. If we're attached to the notion of the self, then we can lose that which we love. We can become entangled with our ego. We can die.

If there is no-self, then there is nothing to become attached to.

How does no-self eclipse the suffering experienced in my leaden thighs as I plod toward the summit of Mount Doug for the second time inside of an hour?

If there is no-self, then there is no separation. If there is no-self, there isn't a man running along a trail on a hill next to the ocean. There is only nature; there is only the totality of creation. There is only one part of nature moving through itself, upward.

And when there is no-self, when there is no boundary

between "me" and "the hill" or "me" and "the forest," it becomes so much easier to draw on the boundless, effortless energy that nature exudes. In Taoism we would say that nature achieves its spectacular existence by "doing little to accomplish much." Trees don't struggle to grow: they just grow. They are humming with energy, with bountiful life.

So might we. And we can draw on their energy to fuel ourselves because it's all the same thing: we simply must dissolve the illusion of separation in order to make use of the energy freely available to us.

When I am running up a long hill past glades of trees, or over the rocky spine of some ancient mountain, I see myself not as separate from the bounty of life around me, but seamlessly a part of it. I actively invite its energy to flow through me. In my mind and my heart, I pull that energy into me and allow it to power me up the trail. It's not an intellectual exercise. I feel this. It is my experience of the world.

I'm not merely replacing one set of "chattering" voices in my head with another, more positive one. When I am moving through the woods, up in the mountains, down in the desert or along the ocean or a creek or river, I let go of the notion that I am separate from that which I am moving through. I surrender. And of course, there is no "I" to do the surrendering.

During these brief moments, born of necessity, there is no duality: there is just creation and it is in motion through itself. It is powered by the same life-giving energy, and it exults in itself.

And then "I" am on the "summit" again. I stride out on the run down through the arbutus, spruce and fir. My focus must remain on the trail, as there are places where a misstep could cause some damage, but the voices have been cast aside, and I let my mind rove a little. The energy that powered me up the side of the hill can also become a portal to the broader creativity of the universe. Here I can recall that I am also a conduit for the universe's desire to express itself. I can make the voices work *for* me.

By the time my run has finished, there is an "I" again, and he's getting in the car to navigate his way home for a shower. The moment of no-self, no-illusion and no-separation fades, and I become absorbed with whatever comes next in my day. But the practice of powering up – of drawing on the world around me for what I need by recalling that there is no "I" to separate me from the world of pure love, pure energy and pure possibility, is one of the most important things I am learning in my search for bliss.

DISCOVERING DHARMA

I don't believe in coincidence. Dictionary.com defines *coincidence* as "something that happens by chance in a surprising or remarkable way." I don't believe that what we perceive as coincidence is mere chance, and I don't think we should be surprised by its occurrence.

Case in point: Earlier this year I lost my part-time job at Royal Roads University. RRU provided good, meaningful work with amazing people in service of a noble cause. Hard times forced the university to make changes, and eliminating my position at the foundation was one of many.

It was no coincidence that only a few weeks previously I'd written a piece called "Conduit," in which I speculated that writing is my dharma. Professionally speaking, it's what I am on this earth to do. It is my purpose. That is what dharma is: it is our purpose in life. That piece of writing was a signpost.

I recall another such crossroads. In the late 1990s I was kicking around the Bow Valley, making a meagre living as a part-time pain-in-the-ass environmental activist and communications consultant, and penning stories for just about anybody who would publish them. Being a freelance writer in Canada, and a chronically underemployed sorta-professional environmental advocate in

Alberta, are two of the least lucrative means by which to earn a living. I figured that by doing both I might double down on a hardscrabble effort.

I remember saying on January 13th, 1999 – my twenty-eighth birthday – that something would have to change. At the end of every month, I had nothing left in the piggy bank. Then I got a call from someone I'd gone to high school with, and who I had run into at a conference in the fall of 1997, asking what I was doing for work. Within a few months I had a choice to make: full-time, gainful and comparatively well-paid employment with an international conservation organization, or continuing trying to scrape together a living as a writer and consultant.

Around the same time, I had coffee with an acquaintance, one of Canada's truly successful freelance writers, Andrew Nikiforuk. I talked with Andrew about my paradox, and he gave me a sage piece of advice: "You can't make *and* report the news at the same time."

I decided to make the news, and so I took a position with Defenders of Wildlife, based in Washington, DC, and helped them set up shop in Canada, which led to the creation of Wildcanada.net, an online activism and grassroots mobilization effort I helped pilot for the next six years.

I continued to write a little, but it wasn't until my time with Wildcanada.net was coming to a close that I began to pursue publishing again. It was the right decision at the time. It was no coincidence that my old school acquaintance called when he did.

Just as today – more than a decade later – it's no coincidence that one of the barriers to writing has vanished. These periods of opportunity seem to move in cycles, and I'm learning to trust them.

Coincidences are an indication of the direction we are supposed to take in life. Put more forcefully, they are a sign from the universe, from God, from the Tao of what we need to do to fulfil our dharma.

I believe that we can will these signposts into existence. I also believe that just as luck favours the prepared, so does coincidence. To be prepared means to be ready to serve. To be prepared means to know what we can do that creates a sense of bliss, and then dedicate ourselves to it. Some believe that success can only be achieved through hard work, and that to be prepared means to have toiled. I believe that many long hours must be logged in service of our dharma, but the bliss we feel as a result of connecting with our life's purpose erases much of the drudgery that may accompany the effort.

Secondly, discovering dharma is a uniquely spiritual experience centred on our service to humanity, to the earth and its creatures. For many it will be about our service to a higher power, be it God, Jesus Christ or the Tao. These are all just words for pure love.

If the energy we radiate is greed, or anger or fear, then we might attract material objects into our lives for a short time, but over the long term, our purpose in life will remain unfulfilled. But if we are serving a higher purpose – if we are serving with love – then discovering our dharma can become a fulcrum with which we leverage our broader spiritual awakening.

Serving with love has been central to my discovery of my dharma. It's helped me to become prepared to follow the signposts when I see them. In the past, fear and anger have acted like blinders to my ability to clearly see signposts. That's starting to change.

I don't purport to have the answer to how we might all become better at creating the signposts, seeing them, and then following them. I can tell you how I have *started*: meditation. Meditation quiets the mind. If our minds are busy, busy, always racing, then it's hard to notice the often subtle indications of direction the universe provides. Meditation is a deep breath in my day. It is a prolonged and refreshing pause.

Meditation also helps create clarity around what it is we really want. My process for creating clarity was to write down a page of things that were really important to me: to have my children in my life on a daily basis; to be a conduit for stories with meaning; to do important work helping people make the world a better place; to find a great love and hold that love close to me.

Even during the most difficult period in my life – during the aftermath of my separation, when my children seemed very far away – I turned to a single page of simple statements as grounding for my meditation. I would read them silently and then I let go of them. Letting go of the outcome is central to this effort. If you have a preconceived notion of how the universe will respond, you'll likely miss important markers along the journey. You'll spoil the surprise.

Meditation is a means by which we can directly connect with the energy and information that is the foundation for everything in the universe. But we must let go of attachment to achieve anything.

Meditation and prayer – stillness – is one means of preparation. It is the yin. The yang is action: in my case it's more than twenty years of writing. It's running. It's being a loving husband and father. It's a lifetime of service.

And so, when my signpost appeared, in the form of a pink slip, I was prepared to act.

It's worth mentioning here that the path isn't always straight. In fact, I doubt it ever is. It's crooked, most often, and a little dangerous. You start inserting your desires into the fabric of the universe and every now and then you're going to drop a thread. My experience is that the universe doesn't just put up a neon sign that says, "Hey, Legault, this way to prosperity and success as a bestselling author," though if wishing made it so....

It's a journey. Faith is crucial to dharma. You must believe in yourself. When you discover your dharma, when you are doing the blissful but often arduous work to

prepare yourself, when you are engaged in the passionate and perilous spiritual journey, you must have faith. You have to believe that you are worthy, and that you deserve to succeed.

I'm writing every day now. I've got two dozen ideas for books in my head, on paper, and in progress. At the same time, I'm relaunching Highwater Mark Strategy and Communications, because serving people who are making the world a better place is an honourable and exciting way of earning a living. Double down again.

And I'm sitting still, trying by not trying to touch the

fabric of the universe and insert a handful of little prayers into the vastness of the Tao.

I don't know what is going to happen next, but I believe that it will be extraordinary, and I'll be ready when it does.

ALREADY HOME

It occurred to me for the first time the other day that I am already home. For more than twenty years I've believed that someday I would reach the apex of the spiritual journey – nirvana, enlightenment – and that I would find myself … well, somewhere, free from worldly suffering. I would arrive at the journey's end like a road-weary traveller, grateful to be finally home. But I've never really been seeking enlightenment. If pressed I would say that what I am seeking is peace.

Just peace; a quiet heart; a moment of freedom from tiresome striving. Freedom from striving for wealth, striving for recognition, striving for health, striving to be loved, striving for well-being, for security. From illusion. Freedom from the promise of enlightenment.

And even freedom from striving for peace.

At times I've worked very hard to find peace. The obstacles have been entirely of my creation, but they have proven to be formidable barriers. For most of my adult life I've been impatient, angry, frustrated and ill-tempered. I've also had a loving heart, and that has helped to balance the equation. At times the passage has been arduous, leaving me disenchanted. If only I knew that I could simply end the search and return to the start. If only I could remember that at those times of disquiet I was as close to peace as I had ever been, then I might have simply sat down on the path and realized I was already home.

When we stop seeking enlightenment, when we cease the wearisome quest for peace, we see that it has been ours from the very start. From the moment of creation, peace has been the gift from the creator. We are already home.

I watch Rio and Silas asleep in their beds, arms splayed above their heads, their faces a perfect reflection of quiet serenity. There is no searching here; there is nothing to strive for.

"Seek nothing and find everything you need," says the *Tao Te Ching*. But we forget. We struggle. We hope to wash ourselves clean of life's anguish with meditation, prayer, stretching before exercise, Brussels sprouts and herbal tea. And it helps. But all striving is a form of suffering, including striving for an end to suffering.

So we return to a clear moment of peace and remember that we have always been enlightened. We have always been pure peace. We are born Buddha and remain Buddha every moment of our life. We've just forgotten.

Maybe enlightenment isn't so crazy a notion, if only I can keep myself from seeking it, and simply experience it, and then let it go.

Father Thomas Keating, of the Christian contemplative movement, says in the movie *One*:

> In the beginning the spiritual journey is the realization, not just the information, but the real interior

conviction that there is a higher power, or God. Or, to make it as easy as possible for everybody, that there is an *Other*. Second step, to try and become the Other. And finally, the realization that there is no *Other*. That you and *Other* are one. Always have been. Always will be. You just think that you aren't.

This doesn't mean that the journey is over. Far from it. It's just starting. But we start knowing that we are already home.

HARNESSING THE
THIRD COINCIDENCE

For the last couple of months, I've been nattering on about discovering my dharma and the coincidences surrounding my departure from Royal Roads University. Somehow my acceptance that writing is what I truly want to do with my life, and the space created for writing by my untimely exodus from my post as a fundraiser for the Bateman Centre, seemed incomplete. There had to be a third coincidence.

One of the first things Jenn and I decided to do when I lost my job was to take a vacation. Liberated from the tyranny of three weeks of holidays each year, we were free to travel, so we headed for the American Southwest. We have both ventured there on numerous occasions, though never together. We planned to spend time riding our bikes and hiking near Moab, venture down the Colorado River and wander into the Maze in Canyonlands National Park, camp on the North Rim of the Grand Canyon and take a quick tour in the vast Escalante.

About a week before Jenn and I left for Utah, I was stirring from my morning meditation when an idea surfaced from my cerebral morass: why am I not writing an environmental murder mystery series set in the Southwest?

Shortly the second book in the Cole Blackwater series – *The Darkening Archipelago* – will go to press. This series is set mostly in Canada. Canada is a very small country. It doesn't publish many books. But the United States, on the other hand – big country, lots of books and book publishers, lots of readers of crime and other genres. I love the Southwest, and have always wanted to write about it.

So I set my intent to have a fully formulated idea for a mystery series set in Utah and Arizona by the time Jenn and I returned from our trip.

Intent is an incredible thing. I've had a lot of practice over the last ten or more years at creating something from nothing. I have come to believe that like everything else, stories are merely a product of the information swirling around the universe, born of an exploding star some ten billion years ago. We humans, with our thick craniums and hyper-developed gift of imagination, are wired to be walking, talking receptors for these stories, and we quickly fashion them into tales about our own extraordinary journey.

I love the creative process. I love taking an idea from inspiration to cultivation. At first there is next to nothing. A single idea: in this case, a terrible, marvellous, beautiful landscape. What do I want to say about such a place? My own niche in the mystery genre is to tell stories that focus on environmental issues. It's what I know the best. There's no shortage of environmental calamities in the

Southwest. How to choose? And how do I create characters and a plot that allows the reader to enjoy a good story without pummelling them over the head with an environmental message (that niche is already filled to overflowing). Who's the protagonist? What makes him or her interesting? Why would a reader want to follow this person through a series of books?

All these questions sloshed around in my head as I was preparing for and departing toward our Utah adventure. Jenn and I talked a lot about the ideas as they began to emerge – like startled, blinking voles from dark fissures in the earth – over the first week of the trip. At first, I didn't want to discuss the ideas *too* much; I feared that if I let them out on their own, they would just slip away. But soon we were yakking for hours – on our hikes in the Maze, over cold beer on the beach at Spanish Bottom, over grilled cheese sandwiches at a riverside café in Mexican Hat – about the narrative arc of the trilogy.

Two-and-a-half weeks into the creative process, I was ready to write it all down. We camped on the North Rim of Grand Canyon for three nights, and choose to forgo long hikes or mountain bike rides for more sedate explorations so I could have the afternoons to sit and scribble. At Point Imperial, with the wind howling and leaves blowing and sun setting, and again on the trail to Wildforss Point, in a grove of golden trembling aspens, I sat and wrote and thought and wrote some more, all the while bouncing ideas off Jenn for perspective.

When we returned home a week ago, I had dozens of pages of notes, including a sketch of how the planned three novels will work together, along with biographical outlines of all the major characters. I've spent a few hours each day over the last week writing as succinct an outline as I am able for the trilogy, and hope to be able to start pitching it to publishers by the end of October.

I have no way of knowing now if the ideas I blurted out in the searing heat of the Maze, or jotted onto paper in the crisp autumn afternoons on the North Rim, will emerge into the literature of the American Southwest. If they do, I have no way to say if anybody will read the books and enjoy them, discuss them with friends, seek out the awe-inspiring landscapes I hope to populate with my characters, and maybe one day stand in a place where the protagonist stood in my imagination and have fiction and fact blur, if only for a moment. (The books will be published by TouchWood Editions through 2016).

What I can say with absolute certainty is this: in just a few short weeks I was able to recognize and harness the power of events emerging and converging, to produce ideas I find exciting and inspiring. This gift is available to us all. We can all tap into this creative power.

If this isn't what I'm supposed to be doing as part of a right-livelihood – the process of earning one's keep while doing good, helpful or ethical work – on this amazing planet, I don't know what is.

TERRAIN-ING

The earth beneath my feet is my best teacher. It provides everything I need in order to learn how to run, and live, fearlessly.

Since injuring my left knee in 2003, I've often been fearful of steep descents; my fear of going downhill extends to my life experience as well. Terrain-ing is how I've overcome that fear. Terrain-ing is the act of letting the trail, its ups and downs, teach you how to run, and how to live.

This fall I'm preparing for a pair of races. The Gunner Shaw, which I've run before, is renowned for the gruelling course it follows over the hills and through bogs and swamps around Thetis Lake. Two weeks later is the Stewart Mountain Challenge, which I've never before participated in. It's a sixteen-kilometre race in the same vicinity, without the sloshing through fetid bogs, but with the added joy of a mad scramble over Stewart Mountain at the apex of the run.

To my surprise, I've discovered that I enjoy preparing for these races because they give me an opportunity to focus my running and my diet on a goal: not finishing last.

As I've said elsewhere, my reason for racing is the sheer masochistic pleasure of running a difficult route through a beautiful natural setting and sharing the experience with a few hundred friends. This fall, however, I've had a bad cold that has lingered for weeks, and it's forced me to forgo much of the prep-work I hoped to do for the Gunner Shaw. With just two weeks to go before the race, I finally get out for a first, easy run. I wind through the streets of Victoria, from my home in Fernwood to Willows Beach, where I pad through the small forested park and then down along the seashore. My lungs labour to draw enough breath, and a couple of times I have to stop because I feel as if I'm drowning on dry land.

When I'm done, I sit down on the living room floor and stretch and pull my copy of *Chi Running* from the shelf. As with so many books in my collection, I've only cracked the spine, but I decide to read it cover to cover now.

Written by ultra-marathoner Danny Dreyer and his wife, Katherine, *Chi Running* teaches how to harness the natural energy of our bodies to make running easier, more efficient and injury-free. I read the book and on a sheet of paper sketch out a two-week training plan to get in shape for the races. I map which runs I will do over the next dozen days, along with a meal plan to maximize the ability of my body to regain its strength after my illness, and build for and recover from my excursions.

My plan is to do another easy run in the next few days, and then gradually build to a series of harder sessions on the Gunner Shaw racecourse in the week before the race itself. My experience with this course is that if you know just how cold and putrid the water will be, you can brace for it. It doesn't elevate the cement-like feeling in the legs – or the reek in the nostrils – but at least you know what you're in for.

In terms of meal preparation, I plan to eat foods intense in carbohydrates for several days before a big training run and before the races themselves, and meals rich in protein – salmon, for me – afterward. I don't want to find myself, as I have in the past, physically incapacitated and emotionally demoralized due to a poor race-recovery strategy. My goal is to rehydrate better and to eat a proper meal after the run in order to help my body repair the damage done to my muscles during the event. That way I can use the Gunner Shaw as a springboard for the Stewart Mountain experience.

The next two runs are on the familiar terrain of Mount Doug, up and over the summit and down through the dark forests toward the sea. Despite the lingering impacts of my cold, I feel pretty good. But I can feel myself holding back as I traverse the summit and start on the steep decline, jumping arbutus roots and using my hands to skim over polished stone.

I turn back to *Chi Running* for advice. I reread the chapter on body posture: the Dreyers advise we use our bodies like a throttle, leaning forward when we want to increase our speed and leaning back to slow down. When ascending the steep hills around Victoria, I have to lean forward five or ten degrees, letting gravity help propel me; when running downhill, I should lean back so that my upper body is parallel with my legs.

But then I read the most important piece of advice yet: relax. Keep my arms and legs loose; run using the bigger muscle groups in my body: thighs, hips and back. Let the smaller muscles, and those more likely to be injured – such as the ones in the knees, calves and ankles – swing loosely. When going downhill, relax and keep the legs loose. In other words: flow.

My next day's run is at Thetis Lake. With this year's racecourse map in hand, I start off at the parking lot and begin to follow the trails through the mist-cloaked woods. The autumn colours are still rich, though their full brilliance has passed. I come to the first climb and try to remember what I read the night before: I lean forward a little, circling my arms loosely as if I were pulling myself up an imaginary rope. I reach the top of the hill and press on, feeling surprisingly good.

I soon come to the first water hazard: a long stretch of swamp that the summer trails avoid but the racecourse bisects. I could go around it. I don't really need to run the rest of this ten-kilometre jaunt with my legs half frozen. But I plunge in, suppressing a yelp, and quickly wade through the mire.

The rest of the run is tough but fun. Lots of rocky uphill climbs and another long, particularly interesting water hazard that involves scrambling over a downed tree in the middle of the swamp. Good fun, and I'm feeling enthusiastic when I come to the last big climb. I know that momentum can be an ally when making my descent, but I have a tendency to get going downhill pretty fast, and it scares the hell out of me.

Over the last few years, I've often found myself going downhill a little too quickly. These have been trying times, and often I've had to confront very difficult emotions: fear, depression, despair. I'm not talking about running downhill anymore, but about *going* downhill. The lessons are the same.

I've had to face the uncomfortable truth that when confronted by those things I fear, I lash out and create a precipitous self-imposed decline. I am aware that I'm going downhill, but every time I struggle against the descent I make it worse.

So down I go; I lean back and relax my body, letting gravity do the work. I use the muscles in my thighs and back and find that I'm gliding over the bulging stones on this pathway, down, down toward Thetis Lake.

Can't I do the same when I feel my anger rise, and find myself in conflict with someone I love? It's the fear of the thing that makes it so difficult to face; the summits are so hard-won and I don't want to lose all the ground I've made and so instead of just accepting that there are always ups and downs in life, I resist. I become rigid. And I get hurt; and hurt others in the process.

Better just to relax. It's just a dip in the trail. Breathe

and let gravity do what it has to do. Don't resist it and don't fight it. This is what my terrain-ing is teaching me.

The earth's ups and downs become my own best coach. I am in training for a race, but what I'm really doing is letting the terrain teach me about life.

Soon the path levels out again and I'm running along the foreshore of Thetis Lake, the woods a marvellous aurora of tan, gold and bronze. The water is flat and calm, and I'm running with ease. I'm feeling ready for the challenges ahead. I still must remind myself when I'm going downhill to breathe, to relax, to stop fighting it every step of the way.

HOLIDAY SHOPPING WITH
THE BUDDHA CLAUS

The Buddha that sits in my entranceway has a tiny Santa hat perched jauntily on his head; set at a rakish angle, it juxtaposes perfectly with Gautama Buddha's serene expression.

I love Christmas. I inherited this from my mother, who worked slavishly to ensure that the season was a flawless expression of the image of her family she projected on the world. Our home was always perfect; presents were piled high under the tree, which itself was cut on our property in Northern Ontario in an idealistic holiday gathering of carolling friends and merriment and dragged home through the waist-deep snow; dinner was an elaborate affair that often induced early forays into eggnog and rum, hold the eggnog.

I love Christmas, but I'm not enamoured with the wild debaucherous consumerism that seems to infect our society like some kind of pathological screwworm, always present but most voracious at this time of the year. But as with all things in life, I live with paradox: I enjoy giving gifts. So I go shopping.

This year I also went in search of the Buddha Claus.

While wandering the downtown streets of Victoria, or

the city's many shopping malls, I tried to imagine what it would be like for a four-year-old to sit on the Buddha Claus's lap and read off their wish list. The Buddha would listen placidly and then, with a warm smile, would explain that much suffering is born from desire and the illusion that "things" can provide us with fulfillment and stave off the inevitable end of the impermanent nature of our transient existence. Then the children would be sent on their way, a copy of the Dhammapada clutched in their sticky fingers.

Maybe the Buddha Claus isn't for everybody.

I spent my albeit brief time in long lines in retail outlets, doing what I could to make the lives of those around me a little better. I gave them the gift of a smile, a friendly word, a feeling of camaraderie, and the so-necessary sense of human connection. I failed at this effort a few times: outside Victoria's biggest shopping mall, I provided unwanted "verbal assistance" to those who failed to grasp that parking lots don't mean that you simply stop unexpectedly and park in the driving lane.

But I hope that in the main I was able to relieve people of a little suffering during what is often a stressful and lonely time of the year. And in doing so, relieve myself of some suffering. It's the illusion of our separateness that so often leaves me feeling unnerved.

As I've said before, the purpose in all my running and my stillness isn't to achieve enlightenment – the permanent end of suffering – but simply to find some peace.

Christ taught us that the meaning of Christmas is peace on earth. The Buddha teaches us that the purpose of life is peace in our troubled souls. We can't have one without the other.

THE ILLUSION OF
FORWARD PROGRESS

This morning I was thinking about progress; about forward progress in particular, and about the illusion of forward progress, to be more specific.

I found myself retracing long-abandoned but familiar steps: the icy trail from staff housing in Lake Louise to the shopping mall where I could buy a *Globe and Mail* and a loaf of bread at Laggan's Deli. Nearly twenty years after my stint as a park interpreter there, I remember those gilded summers as if they were yesterday.

I'm in Lake Louise, ground-truthing some of the scenes in a novel called *The End of the Line,* to be published by TouchWood Editions next year. The book is a historical murder mystery set in what is today Lake Louise, but in the spring of 1884 was alternately known as Holt City, the Summit or Laggan.

When I left Lake Louise late in 1996 – was forced out, actually, buy the park service for being outspoken on the conflict between development and protection in Canada's national parks – I had already been dreaming of being a writer. I return now to work on the fourth draft of a novel, but I'm still a very long way from earning a living at the craft. So much has changed in my life, but

I can't really decide if any of it might be considered forward progress.

What have I learned in all these years, I asked myself, striding across the Pipestone River?

My answer: that the notion of forward progress is an illusion. We believe our lives are on a trajectory from beginning to end, and that time is an arrow that pierces us on its dizzying parabola. But it's not. If it needs a shape at all, it's a spiral, but without a top or a bottom; one that just keeps growing larger and larger as we come to see more about the truth of our existence. Buddhists think of this process as the wheel of dharma, or sometimes simply the wheel of life. Forward progress cannot be measured in material accomplishments – the illusionary hallmarks of modern success – but by overcoming – in fact conquering – those illusions.

I come back to Lake Louise, to the Bow Valley, where I lived for nearly fourteen years, with a few more trips around the circumference of that spiral under my belt. A lot has changed, and a lot has remained the same, and maybe the most important thing is that I know I should not care if I'm making forward progress; only that I'm learning a lot with each turn of the wheel.

THE SOFT SHALL OVERCOME THE HARD

Day breaks over the Continental Ranges; the cold, hard light of dawn edges out the cloudless night. It's minus five but predicted to hit plus twenty today. The remaining snow here in Lake Louise, the highest community above sea level in Canada, will certainly be all but gone come the weekend. Mount Temple, viewed from the window of a friend's home where Jenn and I are visiting, is a familiar sight; it's a triangular, glacier-clad icon that looms more than six thousand feet above Paradise Valley and the Bow Valley. It's my favourite mountain in the world, *so far*. It's hard and angular and imposing, like the landscape that circles it for a hundred kilometres in every direction.

It's an unyielding landscape. It's all perpendicular faces and abrupt edges. It's often very cold, except for a few brief months when it can be very hot. And while the dales that lie like green filaments between the imposing walls of limestone have a gentleness to them, most of this landscape is rigid and obstinate.

It's a hard place on the body. When I lived in the Bow Valley, I felt as if I was always about to crack open. My body itched with the dryness. My head ached from the

Chinook winds that pressed down on the mountains with great regularity.

I remember feeling relief when I moved to the West Coast five years ago. The verdant coastal forests, the soft, rounded hills, the gentle pulse of the ocean; each of these things heralded anabatement to the hardness that had predominated my life.

It was more than physical: I was like the mountains too. Hard, unyielding. I was rigid in my approach to life. The coast and all that has happened in the last five years have helped take the edge off.

The morning sunlight slips down the flank of Mount Temple, illuminating its snow-plastered northern face. I worry that, as I spend more time in this landscape of hard edges and angles, I will take on those characteristics once again myself. In a little less than a year, my family and I will move back to the Bow Valley. Since the day Jenn and I moved her stuff from Canmore to Victoria, we've known we would be back within two years. As you drive a U-Haul truck over snow and ice and winding mountain highways, nothing cheers the soul like the foreknowledge that you'll get to do it again in such a short span of time. That day is drawing close, and I'm trying to figure out how to live once more in such an unforgiving landscape.

"This is the universal truth: The soft shall overcome the hard," says Lao Tzu. I've been preaching this in my work as an activist and as a leader. "All living things are soft and flexible / All things in death are hard and brittle / The hard and the brittle will be broken / the soft and the flexible will endure."

How can I embrace this truth in my own life?

When I moved to the Pacific coast, I felt as if my body relaxed for the first time. Coming home to these mountains doesn't mean I must grow rigid once again. It's no surprise that the answer to this question might be found in water. "Water is as soft as anything on earth / yet mountains and canyons have been sculpted by its force," adds Lao Tzu.

The other day Jenn and I stood at the confluence of the Pipestone and Bow Rivers. When I lived in Lake Louise in the early 1990s, I used to come to this place high up on the Bow River watershed to watch these two rivers seamlessly merge. I dreamed then that my life might emulate this confluence; now I am caught in its joyous flow.

These mountains, of course, have been shaped by water. The frozen sort, the massive glacial ice sheets that covered this landscape in a kilometre of ice ten thousand years ago, gouged the V-shaped valleys into broad, U-shaped dales. We see their work in the sheared-off cliffs and sculpted domes all around us. But it would be a stretch to categorize the last ice age as soft. The last glacial epoch lasted for millions of years and covered much of the northern hemisphere, and I would imagine that to all but the hardiest of creatures it would have seemed unyielding. I don't think it was very relaxing.

Of course, in geologic time, the ice age too yielded to the tilting of Earth and the periodic wobble of its rotation around the sun.

Maybe it's all a matter of temporal perspective.

I think that for my purposes I will look to water's liquid form. See how it moves across the surface of the earth, gently pulling at the stones until they pry loose and succumb to water's patient tug? Watch as it ebbs and flows; sometimes raging in a torrent, pulling entire canyon walls down in the flood, and sometimes placid, a crystal pool as clear as the sky.

"Be at ease," advises Lao Tzu. "When turmoil swirls around you / be as the stone in the river's flow / allow the waters to come and go / come and go."

And be like the water too, soft and yielding and at ease, but with the force and power to move the earth itself. My challenge, when I move back to the Bow Valley, will be to live in a harsh, often unyielding landscape in a way that embodies water's soft strength.

BREAKING THE BUDDHA

My statue of Gautama Buddha broke the other day. Broke *again*, I should say.

I bought this eight-inch-tall statue almost four years ago now, shortly after moving out of my family home and into the hundred-year-old character home in Victoria's Fernwood neighbourhood. I bought it before I had any real furniture or even a wok to cook dinner in. After looking at dozens of different figurines, I selected this particular effigy because of the serene look on "the Conqueror's" face. It was to be a symbol of my new approach to living, and day after day I used it as an *aide-mémoire* for the peace I was hoping to bring into my life.

This statue sits perched in the entranceway, watching over my family as we come and go. Silas and Rio both recognize his placid smile as other children might recognize Big Bird or that crazed purple dinosaur that haunts so many parents' nightmares. When Silas was learning how to build with Duplo, he made his own characters and would present them to me and say, "Look, it's the Buddha." And of course it was.

I keep the Buddha on a ledge that has a slight angle (everything in this old house does), in a prominent place in my entrance, in part to have a touchstone, and in part to announce to those entering and exiting that I am making an effort to clean up my act. The Buddha's prominence is part ego and part beseeching for patience with my indiscretions.

But this house is very old, and more than a little cranky, and is listing precariously to, well, *all* sides at the same time. Put a marble down on any of the century-old Douglas fir floors and off it goes, careening one way and then the next, racing for a wall or stairwell. The doors in the house suffer the most. Their frames are ancient, and the wood is well past its prime, and all the hinges require regular lubrication (don't we all) and every three or four months I have to take them all off, fill in the decaying screw holes and re-hang them.

But sometimes more than three or four months pass and they start to sag and we have to lift the doors to close them properly. And sometimes we don't even do that, and when we pull a door closed a great shudder is sent through the frame as the prehistoric door rattles on its primeval hinges.

And sometimes they get slammed.

Fear is the root of anger. When I get angry I yell, I stomp around, I bolt. I sometimes rush from the house, frustrated and afraid and fuming, not understanding where my anger was born or why it is rearing its head again, but knowing that I have to get away from it. That I have to run from it; that if I can just put enough distance between myself and my fear and my anger, I might finally outrun it.

The door, hanging on its hinges, comes between me and the outside world.

And the Buddha sits on its slanting ledge next to the door.

I can't remember if the first time the Buddha leapt from his ledge I was slamming the door, or just closing it *forcefully* so that it would stay shut.

But I know that the most recent time the Buddha called me to attention was when the door got between me and escape. And down he came. His head broke off, a piece of his shoulder came apart and the funny little pom-pom on his head broke. It stopped me in my tracks.

I stood there looking at him on the ground, trying to feel nothing. Trying to let go of my disappointment with myself. The fact of the matter is that in toppling to the ground, Gautama Buddha alerted me once more to my suffering, and my need to address it. Suffering, according to the Buddha, is the basic human condition. But suffering can be ended, and there is a clear path – the Eightfold Path – to put a stop to it. Enlightenment is the permanent end of suffering. The Buddha is called the Conqueror because he was the first to vanquish suffering and gain as a reward freedom and peace.

I've been walking this path consciously for five or six years. I've been aware of it for much longer than that, trying in my furtive way to ease myself onto this path without actually doing the hard work to address what stands between me and freedom from suffering.

I picked the Buddha up that morning, collecting the little pieces, cradling his decapitated head in my hands, and brought him downstairs to the workbench. He seemed beyond repair that morning. Sometimes everything seems beyond repair. I walked away from him believing that I'd have to throw him out and start over again.

But I didn't.

Sometimes it seems, in my effort to achieve peace, to free myself from the illusions and fears that cloud my vision of reality, that I have to start from scratch again and again. I burn up any progress made over the last half decade – over the last forty years – in the heat of my passions, my anger and my fear.

But the Buddha foresaw this in his own effort to conquer suffering. Anybody who walks a spiritual path does. We take our tentative steps forward, peel back another layer of illusion and come face to face with whatever it is we've hidden beneath the veneer of day-to-day existence. We crack the shell of our illusion to find more illusion. Sometimes it sends us reeling. And when it does, we wonder if we will ever be forgiven; if we will ever truly be free.

All my spiritual teachers would remind me that when I feel as though I have to run away from my fear, from my anger, from suffering – that is the time to sit still. To sit with the ghastly discomfort that surges in my body and makes me want to yell, slam doors and run away.

Gautama Buddha called me to attention: the Teacher

was in the room that morning, and he crashed to the floor so I might relearn a lesson. Once again. There is no ultimate orthodoxy in the path to peace, including the orthodoxy of the Buddha: only the tearing away of illusions and the compassionate, loving embrace of reality, regardless of who we are or what we've done.

I didn't toss my statue of the Buddha in the garbage. Instead I carefully glued his head back in place, even delicately bonding the little pom-pom back atop his tranquil head. We don't have to start over; we can start so much further down the path, and we can be forgiven our indiscretions and transgressions along the way.

But I am going to find a better place for my statue. Just to be on the safe side.

TRAIL NOTES: PART FOUR

What thing beyond your control
are you worrying about?

What bubbles have you created around
yourself? Can you pop one of them?

What purpose are you on earth to fulfill?

What patterns are you willing to interrupt to
create new behaviours that make you happier?

If you could quiet the voices of doubt,
what would you be able to do?

What simple act can you perform today
to relieve someone else's suffering?

PART FIVE

Downhill through Forests

The trail drops away below us. The sun drapes golden light across the canopy of maple, oak and dogwood. We can let go and let our legs carry us swiftly along the trail that weaves down through the forest.

Two years of planning comes to a close as my family and I move back to the Bow Valley.

After twenty years of trying to publish books, I find an editor and a publisher who supports my work and shares my literary vision.

The reality of having to find new work to pay the bills, however, puts a new twist on all my talk about dharma.

Meditation, study and teaching about the path to ending suffering are the cornerstones of my practice. Writing is the vehicle I use to teach about my own karmic journey, and my furtive steps to conquer suffering.

OUR BRIEF LIVES BENEATH
THE OCEANIC SKY

Maybe it's a once-in-twenty-five-years event.

The last time I had the dream, I was sixteen. I got up and went about my morning, making my way to M.M. Robinson High School in Burlington much as I did every other day. My presence in the halls felt oddly detached, even more than usual. I recall wandering as if directionless, not certain which class I was supposed to attend or where my friends were. At one point I recall touching the face of a friend and saying goodbye.

Then I was in my buddy Greg's car, in the passenger seat, while other friends crowded in the back. I could hear them laughing, carrying on as we often did, but I was apart from it, watching Hamilton's industrial skyline from the Skyway bridge. The world beyond the windows of the car passed in a translucent kaleidoscope of light and colour. I knew that Greg wasn't driving me home; I was travelling toward whatever comes after death. I didn't feel panic or fear, just sadness that this life was over. The feeling was oddly peaceful.

I awoke in tears; it was the last time I woke my mother up after a nightmare.

Fast-forward nearly twenty-five years. I'll be forty in a few months. Now I cradle my own children in my arms when they awake in tears.

I'm dreaming again: it's my birthday party, hosted by my friend Jason Meyers and his partner, Brianne. Other friends are there. There is music and light and colour. Someone says that we're going to sing and Brianne picks up her guitar and I'm excited because I love music. But the moment is cut short, and I realize it's not my birthday. It's my funeral. Jenn is there and she's holding my hand and I don't want to let go but I don't have any choice. And I can feel that same calm sadness in my gut that I did more than half a lifetime ago. The feeling has a *signature* that I'll remember forever. And I am thinking as I let go that I thought I'd have more time.

When I awake she is with me. Jenn thinks the nightmare is about the kids and says that they are fine and that she just checked on them. I tell her my dream and repeat that I just didn't want to say goodbye so soon.

I'm halfway through the journey. Maybe more. And there's still so much to do. I feel as if I'm just getting started. And I'm not ready to say goodbye yet.

I remember my favourite quote, from Edward Abbey's *The Fool's Progress*: "I want to weep, not for sorrow, not for joy, but for the incomprehensible wonder of our brief lives beneath the oceanic sky."

Maybe it's a once-in-twenty-five-years event. A reminder, as if I needed one, that life is short, and there is a lot to do, and many, many people to love, and that I am blessed beyond words to be alive.

WHY MOVE AGAIN?

In the early 1990s I was keenly interested in the idea of bioregionalism: the premise that political, cultural and environmental systems could be based on naturally defined areas called bioregions, or ecoregions. Bioregions can be defined by physical and environmental features, including watershed boundaries and soil and terrain characteristics. I had read and reread Kirkpatrick Sale's groundbreaking 1985 book on the subject, *Dwellers in the Land,* and remember clearly his definitive advice to those wishing to make the world a better place: *You must not move. Find a place that feels halfway like home and stay* (I quote from memory). The idea being that people who affix themselves in place will work to better that place, and defend it, and when home is defined by natural borders, such as a river valley, we make decisions that tend to improve rather than despoil it.

I spent the better part of a year – while living in Lindsay, Ontario – planning various bioregional activities; I even helped start a magazine called the *Root* that celebrated life in the Kawartha Bioregion. And then I moved. I got the call that my seasonal position as a park naturalist in Banff National Park was starting, so I packed up my bags and hopped a flight for Calgary and never again considered the Kawartha Lakes my home. That was at least eight moves ago, but most of those have been within the Bow Valley, with the exception of the six months spent on the South Rim of the Grand Canyon in 1993–94, and the last five years I've spent on Vancouver Island.

And now it's time to go again. When Kat and I moved to Victoria in May 2005, my world was very different. Having spent the better part of fourteen years in the Bow Valley, my family and I were looking for a change. Kat had family in Victoria, and my best friend, J, was finishing his PhD at UVic, so the coast made sense. I'd always dreamed of living by the ocean, and this seemed like a good place to raise children.

Almost immediately after moving to Victoria, I began to miss the mountains. Tiny *refugia* such as Mount Doug and Mount Work were fine for running, but what I

craved was wildness. Big, open ranges of mountains such as those in Strathcona were just too far away to be a part of my daily life.

Kat and I separated a year or so after Silas was born. A year after that, I fell in love with Jenn – and Kat with Andy – both of whom we imported from the Bow Valley.

We all missed the mountains, and small-town life, and the wildness of having Banff National Park and Kananaskis Country – a four-thousand-kilometre matrix of mountains and foothills, parks and multiple-use areas – as our back yard. So we came to an agreement: all six of us would move back to Alberta when the time was right. That was three years ago now. We've been actively planning the move for the last two.

It's a leap of faith. Canmore, Alberta, is a small town,

and though we have a lot of friends there, both Jenn and I are leaving very close friends behind. As a consultant, I've worked with more than thirty-five businesses, governments and non-profits since starting Highwater Mark upon arriving in Victoria, but only two of those have been Alberta-based. Job prospects in that town are better than in most centres of twelve thousand people, but they are still limited. And the more trying aspects of living in the Bow Valley – very long, cold winters, and the reality that the town is very much entrenched in Alberta's wildly conservative politics – makes living there difficult at times.

But it feels like home. In the five years since I left, I've come to realize that the change I was looking for when I left the Bow Valley wasn't what was outside my four walls, but was inside me. What was making me unhappy – in my relationships, in my choice of places to live and in my vocation – wasn't anybody or anything else: it was me. I've just started the hard work to address my fear, my anger and my suffering. Being back in a place that feeds my soul's yearning for wildness will help.

The Bow Valley is where the four adults who are working hard to raise two beautiful children can all agree that we can live in peace. Jenn and I were married in the adjacent Spray River Valley last year, and our fantasy is to spend the next part of our lives together exploring, and re-exploring, the sublime splendour of snowy mornings on a Nordic track, and long summer days high in the alpine.

It's not going to be easy to say goodbye to Vancouver Island. Jenn's parents live in Nanaimo, and they have become a regular part of Silas's and Rio's lives. I'll miss watching the boys running on the beach, and I'll miss running along the ragged coastline, or up and over the region's forested hills with J. I'm looking forward, however, to sharing with the boys the comfort that wilderness is as essential to the human soul as food and water is to the body, and love is to the heart. We can leave the Big Island behind knowing that it's only a day's drive away, and that our lives are richer for these past five years.

There is no guarantee that this move is the last. I've stopped making such pronouncements. But the Bow Valley, as Kirkpatrick Sale says, *feels halfway like home*. It's a community of good people who care about one another and about the land that defines them. It's where Jenn and I feel complete. It's time to head back over the mountains and set down some roots and see what grows.

THE PATH THROUGH
THE WOODS

For almost three years I felt as if I was saying farewell to Victoria. Given that I lived there for five-and-a-half years, that's a long goodbye. The moment finally came, and on the last day of November, we began to cram the contents of our Victoria home into the truck, and several days later finally closed the door on that chapter of our lives. I drove the U-Haul and Jenn piloted our aging but trustworthy Nissan pickup; the Subaru was left behind for another stage of the complex logistics. We made Canmore in two days of white-knuckle driving – including fishtailing the twenty-six-foot-long rental on black ice on the west side of Golden – that had both of us swearing that we'd never do it again. We arrived in the Rockies under cold, clear skies.

The truck was unloaded with the help of friends working in shifts, and after three nights in our new home, I flew to Bozeman, Montana, and then back to Victoria to pick up the kids after their last day of school. As the boys and I walked to the car, Rio said to me: "I can't believe we're doing this right now." I knew how he felt.

Then we did the drive again, this time minus the ass-heavy truck, and with clear and dry roads.

In between there were three days of final farewells in that coastal enclave that for five years we had called home. It seemed appropriate that the days were heavy and overcast, with rain coming in fits and spurts. On Thursday, however, the day dawned brightly, and after dropping the boys at school I made my way to Mount Doug for what would be my final run over that rocky hill's forested slopes.

As I've said elsewhere, in the time I spent in Victoria, I probably ran over Mount Doug a thousand times, in all likelihood many more. As I wove my way up through the dense, perfumed cedar and Douglas fir forest, I recalled that during my first week in Victoria I was so sad about leaving the mountain wilderness behind, but the discovery of tiny Mount Doug buoyed my flagging spirits. Here was a place that at least was natural, though by no means wild, and certainly not wilderness.

Mount Doug became my sanctuary. Like other urban woodlands before it – and here I think of the unintentional but often appreciated forests behind my teenage home in Burlington – it became a buffer between the madness of city life and my own wild heart.

On Mount Doug I experienced some of my greatest insights over the last five years. While running through its sun-dappled woods I experienced – not just intellectually, but in actual practice – the dissolution of the boundary between myself and the world around me. I can recall the place on the trail where I first felt the sensation I describe as *bliss*. I could see everything at once, feel everything, taste and hear everything – because, of course, I *was* everything at once. The feeling of peace washed over me and carried me along the trail in an effortless glide that I've become addicted to, and seek to experience again and again. And I do.

Mount Doug was the place where I most often went to run with J. He'd push me as we ran up the steep rocky flanks of the hillside, talking all the way, circling through its Garry oak forests, and racing down its egresses toward the sea. We covered hundreds of kilometres, maybe a thousand, over the five years we ran there together, and continued to build a friendship that will, no doubt, last a lifetime. Saying goodbye to J and his family was, beyond a doubt, the hardest thing about leaving Victoria.

Mount Doug was also where, on a strange day in late July 2006, I experienced the darkest moments in my life so far. It was while running through those cherished woods that I had my closest brush with mortality yet: the belief that only suicide could end my pain. It was there that I realized I was in mortal danger if I didn't make changes in my life – and so I did, and still am.

It has been a long trail. And a good one. And sometimes very hard. New life and old fears and dark anger lay among the salmon and the cedar on the path from the sea to the summit. The discovery that life isn't necessarily supposed to be sad – and that peace truly is *every step*, as the Buddhist monk Thich Nhat Hanh says – was made with each plodding footfall. I discovered too that peace, of the heart and of the soul, must be rediscovered each day with a commitment to experiencing without fear the steep rises and rocky plunges on this path through the sacred, ephemeral woods we call our lives.

At last I came once more to the bald, round summit and looked again over the forested city of Victoria, and beyond it the circling sea and the chains of mountains. It was a perfect, clear day: even Mount Baker, one hundred miles distant and often shrouded in cloud on a sunny morning, stood in sharp contrast against the azure sky. This place, this hill, these people have served my family well, and we have loved them, and now as we take our leave, I am grateful. I turned and bowed in the four directions, offering my heartfelt thanks to the earth, sea and

sky, and to those who have blessed Rio, Silas, Jenn and me with their love and friendship this past half decade.

And lastly I bowed in the direction of my future: toward the east and the Rocky Mountains. I set off down the path at a fair clip, the way ahead unfurling at my feet, the long trail disappearing through the woods and toward a future alight with the promise of hope, of love and of peace.

40/9

Rio and I have birthdays two weeks apart. I turned forty in the middle of January. Rio turns nine today. Passing the fortieth milestone seemed like a pretty big deal at the time, but now that it's two weeks in the rear-view mirror, its significance has faded. At the time, Jenn and I were in southern Mexico, in the Yucatan; we spent the day driving from the Caribbean coast to the Gulf of Mexico. We stopped in Chetumal, the state capital of Quintana Roo and the setting of my novel *Thicker than Blood*, to do on-the-ground research, and then pressed ourselves for almost six hours of exhausting driving to reach Campeche on the Gulf Coast.

Along the way we had a lot of time to talk, and I remember telling Jenn about my fears that my life's journey was half over. If I took care of myself, and if luck was on my side, I might get another forty or fifty years out of this corporeal being that houses heart, head and soul.

There is still so much to do.

Back in Alberta, in our glorious home, Jenn throws me a slow-motion surprise party. The guests – many old friends who I have lost touch with while in BC – show up over the course of an hour or two, and I'm grateful that I put on a party shirt for the occasion. Silas and Rio run wild with half a dozen other kids, and the party feels like equal parts house-warming and birthday celebration.

I remember my mother's fortieth birthday as if it were yesterday: making her a card with a hand-drawn picture of a glamorous woman reclining on a sports car, the sentiment being that she was still young at forty, even though I thought she was ancient at the time.

A few days later, the morning dawns on Rio's ninth birthday, the beginning of his tenth trip around the sun, and it feels so right to be back in Canmore, where he was born.

I lie in bed with my boy, his little brother still asleep in the bunk above us, and he tells me about his nighttime dreams. We discuss why we dream, and what nightmares are, and why we are afraid of some things and not others. And then he tells me about his real dreams, the ones that he will pursue in life. He wants to travel around the world. He wants to work with animals. He wants to climb mountains. He wants Star Wars Lego for his birthday. And carrot cake.

We rise and get ready for the day, and he and I sneak off and have breakfast together in town before I drop him at school. It feels so right to be here.

Later today we'll take the boys to the Nordic Centre for their ski lessons and then head to Boston Pizza for a birthday dinner. Rio wants to go to the Royal Tyrrell Museum to see the paleontology exhibits, so the next nice weekend they are here, we'll make the trip to Drumheller.

Part of what sends jolts like electricity through me from time to time is the knowledge that even as we plan and prepare for our lives here in the Rocky Mountains, things are slipping away. Rio has recently started to greet me with hugs when I pick him up from school again, but I expect that will be short-lived. Soon it will be back to fist-bumps as a means of acknowledging my aching love for him as he makes his way into the world. Silas is still all snuggles and hugs, but the cruel reality of being a parent is that from the moment your children are born – the very first moment – you have to start letting go.

As it is with our very own lives: it's all just a process of letting go, of surrender.

This year will be a big year, for the nine-year-old and the forty-year-old. I recently learned that my amazing publisher, TouchWood Editions, will pick up my third mystery series, essentially publishing my books as fast as I can write them.

It seems that the return to the Bow Valley, to the Rocky Mountains, has indeed been fortuitous. And of course, there will be a world to travel. And animals to help. And mountains to climb.

And Star Wars Lego. And a carrot cake.

ENTERING THE
(COSTCO) MARKET

In the Zen Buddhism tradition, after one has attained enlightenment, one returns to the world with helping hands, easing the suffering of others and helping them follow the way of the Buddha. This is called Entering the Marketplace, and is the culmination of the Ten Oxherding Pictures, a parable on the path to enlightenment.

Let me be clear about this from the start: I've skipped over steps four through nine and rushed headlong and willy-nilly into the Market. There will be more on that later.

My first time in a Costco, to do anything more than gawk in stunned amazement, was on December 23rd, 2010. It was pretty exciting. Jenn and the boys and I had just moved into our new home in Canmore, Alberta, and had resolved to investigate the option of buying some of our staples in bulk to save money.

During our time together in Victoria, Jenn always threatened to drag me to Costco, just a few kilometres away in Colwood, to stock up on things we used a lot of: flats of juice and cases of Almond Breeze were the examples she suggested. Now, with the nearest Costco a solid hundred kilometres down the road in Calgary, we decided to finally visit one. We did this on the second-to-last day before Christmas. For some, this might sound like a recipe for disaster.

It likely would have been, five years ago. And it likely would have been had I not been to India in 2009. But a lot has happened in the last five years; I've done a lot of work, the sort of work that allows me to step into a Costco store teeming with humanity and see it as an opportunity to make people's lives a little easier. Where else could I find so many opportunities to greet so many other human souls? And get little blocks of cheese on fancy crackers for free as a reward?

For most of my life, and for the last five years or so, I've been trying steadfastly to find an end to my suffering, which is characteristic of all human endeavours. The Buddha taught that, simply put, life entails suffering. Some mistake this as reading that life *is* suffering. That's not what Gautama Buddha taught. What he said was that in life, there is suffering. He also taught that there is a cause to that suffering, and that among the root causes of suffering are attachment and our failure to understand the reality of our universe, which is that we are all connected to one another.

Costco is a good place to look if you want to find people who are suffering. Walmart too. We rush up and down the aisles, scanning the case lots for something, anything, that will provide us with the illusion of relief from what causes us pain. Inside we feel an ache:

loneliness, isolation, separation. We mistake these *things* we are purchasing for our true source of comfort. We believe that if we just had a flat of juice or a case of Almond Breeze in the cupboard, then we'd be satisfied. But of course we're not. Because we drink the damn things and then we need more.

I wandered around Costco, following my wife up one aisle and down another, loading up the cart with all the things that we regularly buy – from rice to cereal to loaves of bread – and greeting people with the same phrase: "This is my first time in Costco, how about you?"

People would smile and say hi and a few would laugh and we'd strike up a conversation. We'd talk about Christmas plans and the kids and the Calgary winter and then we'd both move on.

"We are all so much together," said the philosopher and theologian Albert Schweitzer, "but we are dying of loneliness." I believe I can see this in people's faces, in the distracted way they move through the world. Telling people that it was my first time in Costco was my way of chipping away at that loneliness, and dissolving the illusion of separation. Suddenly the shell around us cracks, and we become human again: we connect, and for a moment the bubbles we create to protect our fragile souls from the challenges of the world pop.

When Jenn and I got home from Costco, it felt good to fill up the cupboards with the necessities of life. Two cases of Almond Breeze and a double-sized box of

Cheerios means fewer trips to the local Safeway, and more money to pay for the other necessities of life. I don't think there's anything wrong with that, so long as we're being conscious about what we buy. But let's not mistake that feeling of temporary comfort for the permanent relief from suffering that the Buddha taught was possible.

In Zen, the Oxherding Pictures are an allegory on enlightenment. There are hundreds of versions of this fable online and in books, and each is illustrated with simple, eloquent line drawings or watercolours. I base the interpretation which follows on Roshi Philip Kapleau's book *The Three Pillars of Zen*.

One: Seeking the Ox. Even though the Ox has never gone astray, we search for it, forgetting the true source of peace. Instead we mistake worldly gain and fear of failure for our true path.

Two: Finding the Tracks. Through the sutras and teachings of the Buddha we come to learn about the Ox. Though still living in the mist of illusion, we know that there is another path.

Three: First Glimpse of the Ox. We realize that everyday distractions are blinding us from seeing the Ox. We catch our first glimpse of him through a brief parting of the mist of illusion.

And for the record, after twenty years of study and five years of challenge and practice, I think I've *just started* to glimpse reality. The hard, sometimes deeply painful work of step four yet eludes me.

Four: Catching the Ox (or, as Cat Stevens put it: Catch Bull at Four). After some effort, we are able to rope the Ox, but it is wild, and is attached to its old habits, so struggles. We must use patience and courage to hold onto what we have caught.

Five: Taming the Ox. The struggle with the Ox is won: we have conquered suffering. We no longer struggle with our true nature, but instead accept it, and smile at the paradox of existence. We overcome delusion, accept and triumph over attachment and harbour no illusion of separation.

Six: Riding the Ox Home. Serene, we are no longer in conflict over "gain" and "loss." Though temptations still ply us, we remain undisturbed.

Seven: Ox Forgotten, Self Alone. In the dharma – our purpose in the universe – there can be no separation between ourselves and others, ourselves and the world around, and ourselves and enlightenment. This is in part because there *never was* any separation; it's only our thinking, and the delusion that this creates, that make us believe we are alone.

Eight: All Forgotten. All attachment is vanquished, including attachment to holiness, and to being the Buddha.

Nine: Returning to the Source. We have never been separated from enlightenment. We are already home; we are already a part of the source, we always have been.

Ten: Entering the Marketplace with Helping Hands.

Having seen past the illusion and having conquered suffering, our work now is to help others find the tracks of the Ox and embark on their own passage.

I don't think we need to wait for steps four through nine to occur in order to cut straight to the desire to enter the Marketplace with helping hands. As I've said elsewhere, I'm not always successful. I'm still impatient and hot-headed and have a temper and sometimes I'm not very nice. When I catch myself behaving this way – behaving as if the people I'm curt with aren't simply an extension of my own fearful, fragile self – I make a point now of apologizing and remembering the greeting of Namaste: two sprits greeting one another; we are the same thing.

On a more recent visit to Costco with Rio and Silas, we did our shopping and I explained to them my approach to visiting Costco, and when we were done we proceeded toward the checkout. The long lines stretched back toward the cases of impulse items: chocolate bars and twelve-packs of socks. I felt a wave of panic that I'd just loaded hundreds of dollars of food into my shopping cart and that there were people in this world who would never see such a bounty. I looked around me and felt a wave of pity (that most regrettable of emotions) for all the people who look tired and sad and lonesome. And then I looked behind me in the lineup and saw such a face: two faces, a couple, who looked worn and weary.

"Hi," I said, and smiled. "How are you?"

But what I really meant was: *You are not alone.*
"How was your day today?"
You and I are one.
"I hope that you have a good night. Take care…."
You are loved. I love you. Find peace.

WATER TONGLEN

It's Friday afternoon and the sun has returned to the Bow Valley. The final patches of snow have disappeared from the matrix of trails in the dark pine benches above Canmore. The sun is a welcome relief. But at the same time as I salute its arrival, I say goodbye to something far more precious: my sons.

I'm about to start three weeks of frenetic travel, almost all of which will see me out of the country, travelling around Montana and Wyoming, and on to Victoria for a crime-writing conference, and then, after just two days back in Alberta, back to Montana once again.

The thought of it makes me dizzy. The prospect of seeing my children for just two days over the next three weeks makes me feel ill.

I drop Rio off at school on Friday morning, and ask him to look at my eyes, and tell him how much I love him. And then he is gone, nine years old and confident and already so focused on his own challenges. Next is Silas; I take him to his daycare provider and spend a moment with him in my arms, and then he is gone too, waving and smiling and growing weary of so many *I love you*s.

Children simply don't project forward in time the way we do as adults. It's a trick I'd like to relearn.

I grope my way to my pickup and close the door and

let tears momentarily win the battle. After a moment, feeling as if I was in some country and western song, crying in an aging pickup, I straighten and tell myself to "toughen up." Others, I remind myself, go months without seeing their kids. I just need to stay "frosty" about this absence.

By late in the afternoon I'm feeling anything but tough, so I do one of two things I do when I am feeling defeated (the *other* is drink beer and mope): I head out to run the trails above my home in the Bow Valley to let sweat and bone and muscle work through my dark ennui.

It's my first snow-free run of the year, and it feels good. Nature has always been my tonic. It's where I have always turned for solace during difficult times in my life. When the Buddha sought to end suffering in his own life, he sat under the Bodhi tree and meditated. There, the demon Mara came to temp him with the trappings of attachment and pleasure, and when Gautama Buddha resisted, Mara asked – as his final effort to wrench enlightenment from the man who had been Siddhartha – "Who will be your witness?" Who would observe, and thereby validate, the Buddha's freedom from suffering with everlasting enlightenment? The Buddha, his fingers trailing on the soft ground beneath him, simply said: "The earth will be my witness."

And so it was.

So the earth bears witness to my own suffering as I run past the open aspen glades and dark pines along the base of Grotto Mountain. After some time, I come to one of the deep fissures that are the namesake of this mountain: a dell cut into the side of the peak where a seasonal stream courses. Normally I take the long, steep trail down along the edge of this grotto, but this day the sound of water floats up through the trees and is like a clarion call.

I run down the path, the temperature dropping as I reach the tiny watercourse, and know exactly what I must do. Once on the water's edge, I weave my way up the tiny creek – just a few feet wide and so clear – to find a set of waterfalls, each dropping four or five feet and performing the most perfect music of nature.

Sitting on the bank, I draw in a deep, moisture-laden breath and exhale my sadness. I can feel the erosion of the hardness that I have tried to use to guard myself. As with the stones in its path, water can work its patient ways against the most stalwart barrier we erect between our hearts and love and compassion.

I realize this tiny waterway has borne on its back another gift: connection.

In Buddhism, the practice of tonglen is a means by which we can connect with others: friends, loved ones and perfect strangers.

Pema Chödrön says this:

> The tonglen practice is a method for connecting with suffering —ours and that which is all around

us— everywhere we go. It is a method for overcoming fear of suffering and for dissolving the tightness of our heart. Primarily it is a method for awakening the compassion that is inherent in all of us, no matter how cruel or cold we might seem to be."

The sound of the rivulet fills my ears, and then my heart. For a moment I imagine that I can hear the voices of every other soul who is sad and missing someone. I can hear them saying goodbye, and experiencing the ache of separation and the despair of loss.

I think of my own father, who when I was young travelled on business for a week at a time and was often away.

I think of soldiers serving overseas, bidding their families goodbye for months – years – at a time. Imagining their children growing up without them; not knowing when, or if, they will ever come home.

And then I am connected to those who have committed some terrible crime, and who are locked away and who leave families behind. They too must miss their children, knowing that they may never get to hold them in their arms again.

Water is the blood of the earth, and the creeks and rivers its circulatory system. Every drop of water that rushes past me on Grotto Mountain is connected to every other drop around the world. This water tripping down the Eastern Slopes of the Rocky Mountains was once in the Euphrates River in Babylon, and in the Great Lakes, and somewhere in the vastness of the Pacific Ocean. To sit by its side and feel the coolness on the tips of my fingers is to touch everything all at once.

These waters flow past the sadness, the suffering, that everyone else on earth experiences; the loss, the sorrow of saying goodbye, and often, though not always, the bliss of reunion. This water connects me to every other person's suffering, and I can feel love and compassion for them, as I must for my own temporary sadness. I resolve that over the next three weeks, when I feel the suffering of being apart from my children, I will not build armour around my heart but instead allow myself to remain connected, through the water tonglen, to my own suffering and that of others.

After a while, my legs stiff with lactic acid, I rise and shake them out and run up the steep hill, the sound of the water still pulsing in my ears. I'm halfway through my run, but already I feel better, my armour left in a pile by the tiny creek to melt back into the woods, the earth beneath my feet bearing silent witness, my head not so self-obsessed with my own troubles. Another thirty minutes of up and down through the spring forest and I'll be home. Then I can have a beer and determine not to mope.

LIGHTEN UP

One year ago my family and I moved into our home in Canmore, Alberta. Three hundred sixty-five days seem to pass very quickly, and now, in many ways, the five-and-a-half years I spent on the coast feel dreamlike in their signature.

In a nearly comical way, I continue to ruminate on the extraordinary journey. The part of the adventure that still makes me laugh, in a nervous, slightly manic way, was the extraordinary effort to haul all our stuff across the mountains from Victoria back to Canmore. Fishtailing into oncoming traffic in a fully loaded, twenty-six-foot-long U-Haul van on black ice on a mountain road has a way of sharpening the mind.

Five years ago I had almost no possessions. Everything I owned fit in a friend's Delica van. When I moved into the big old Victorian house on Chambers Street in Fernwood, the place was practically empty. It felt pretty good.

Over the next few years, it filled up. Old third-hand furniture was discarded for better, second-hand stuff. The bed I built for Rio and Silas was replaced by two beds bought at a garage sale. As if by spontaneous cellular division, children's socks, toys and outdoor gear just materialized. When Jenn and I moved her possessions from Canmore to Victoria for our two years there, we unloaded a medium-sized U-Haul into the house, and it started to feel like a home.

By the time we were ready to move our combined lives back to Canmore last December, we had to rent the largest U-Haul on the lot, and we still made dozens of trips to Value Village to unload our unwanted processions.

I get attached to things. They represent comfort, security, and ease. But they also act as talismans for memories. Before I made the move from Victoria back to the mountains, I got it in my head that I would expunge some of these mementos from my life. I had this notion of throwing something away every day for 180 days to symbolize turning around 180 degrees.

That's the way I imaged our move back to the Rockies. Turning around completely; leaving old patterns, old habits, old fears and old attachments behind. I threw a lot of stuff away. I wish I had kept a list, but that too would have been just another damn thing to keep track of, and I didn't need that. I think the most significant thing I discarded during that time was a clay statue that had been sculpted and given to me by my first significant girlfriend, back when we were in high school. It had broken several times over the last twenty-two or -three years, and I'd glued it back together. For me it represented an attachment to my past that I had to discard to fully embrace the present. It left without ceremony.

When it came time to finally load the U-Haul, we

were overwhelmed with the amount of stuff we still had. It took two-and-a-half days to load the truck. The first three-quarters were easy. The last quarter took a day-and-a-half. By the end, I resorted to rigging a net of yellow rope to hold all the stuff in. And then we loaded our pickup: plants, cleaning supplies, the third coffee maker, and other random things we couldn't let go of. "Why are we holding on to all this stuff?" I kept asking myself, and random passersby.

Why indeed? Some of our things provide us with necessary comforts, like the toaster, the first coffee maker, the teapot and the corkscrew. We need some things to live day to day, to earn a living, to enjoy our time with our families and friends. But much of the stuff jammed and jimmied into the back of the U-Haul, like much of what we surround ourselves with in modern society, isn't needed to enjoy our lives; it comes between us and our ability to live fully.

The mass of accumulated possessions in modern life forces us into a sort of spiritual indentured servitude and insulates us from the real world. We must work like dogs to afford all the things we think will give us pleasure: TV screens the size of fridges, cars the size of armoured vehicles, a basement full of toys, gadgets, equipment and memorabilia. Some of it is useful. Much of it is clutter, under our feet and in our hearts. It holds us down and ties us to the past and creates barriers to living fully in the present.

Why hold on to it all? Four reasons, I think: First, because we are afraid of being uncomfortable. Second, because we are attached to our past. Third, because we are afraid of confronting our own suffering. Fourth, because we are afraid of our impermanence – we are afraid to die.

Our things give us physical comfort. Some of them make our lives easier. But at what cost? In addition to the slavish labour we must undertake day in and day out to afford the things that supposedly make our lives better, many of these so-called comforts distract us from the true source of our discomfort, and keep us from confronting our own fears. What are we so afraid of that we must distract ourselves for so much of our lives?

All the stuff in our lives keeps us looking backwards. Reflection on and celebration of our personal history is wonderful. But there comes a time when we have to let it go. Too often we hold onto things long after they have served their purpose. Too often, rather than living in the present, we surround ourselves with mementos of a time of our lives that no longer serves us.

Suffering is a fact of life. We all suffer. Suffering is overcome with the practice of daily meditation, purposeful living and practicing loving-kindness, among other tenets of the Eightfold Path. Too often we don't even realize the depth to which we suffer because we're distracted. We watch TV, or listen to our iPods, or amass untold numbers of gadgets that keep us from sitting quietly and reflecting on the true purpose of our lives: to overcome suffering, and to help others do the same.

And then there is death. We are possibly the only creatures on earth who are aware, from a very early age, that we will die. Our things serve the purpose of insulating us from the inevitability of impermanence. They distract us from the suffering caused by this knowledge, persuade us that we needn't face this fear and surmount it, and convince us that maybe we will cheat death if only we can protect ourselves from the world with our processions.

This has been on my mind for the last year. Why all this stuff? Like many others, I've had fantasies of throwing it all in the dump (or having a nice big bonfire), strapping my backpack on and disappearing to some remote corner of the world, taking with me just a little bit of the stuff. But that would only be a temporary solution. In a few years, there would be more stuff once again.

And I like my things. Jenn and I have a small, tasteful home filled with books and keepsakes from our travels, and photos that have meaning. The solution isn't external. It's not about the world that surrounds me, cluttered or otherwise. It's about the world within.

There is a wonderful scene in the Pixar movie *Up*. The story tells of a deeply unhappy older gentleman, Carl, and an enthusiastic boy named Russell, who take a tremendous journey by tying thousands of balloons to Carl's house and flying, dirigible-fashion, to South America. The house is filled with memories of Carl's deceased wife,

Ellie. While alive, she and Carl dreamed of adventure and visiting Paradise Falls, but instead lived a quiet, even contented, life. When Ellie died, Carl was wracked with guilt for failing to fulfill his wife's dream.

Toward the end of the movie, one of Carl and Russell's tagalongs, a ten-foot-tall bird named Kevin, is in trouble. In order to come to his aid, the duo have to get the house airborne again. But Carl is unable to let go of all the memories entangled there, and all the physical reminders of his wife keep the house mired on the ground. Furious, Russell departs to help Kevin on his own, leaving Carl to confront his memories. In a moment of clarity, Carl realizes that all the things that he believed mattered are weighing his house down, so he throws them all out the front door. Last to go are the symbolic chairs that he and his wife sat in throughout their marriage. The balloons lift the house off the ground and Carl flies to both Kevin's and Russell's rescue. Carl has learned that his past was keeping him from living in the present.

Does this mean that I'll be throwing more of my books and photos, my beloved mountain bike and my furniture out the window this weekend? No. But I am aware of how all the things in my life tie me to my past, and distract me from addressing what is truly important. I've made a commitment to lighten up, both physically and emotionally, so that spiritually I can strive for some manner of freedom from suffering.

THE PRAYER TREE

There is a tree on one of the grassy benches above my home in Canmore that is sacred. It's a stalwart Douglas fir that rises up just a little taller than the other fir and spruce that surround it. From its base you get the standard tremendous view of the Bow Valley, the Three Sisters, Mount Lougheed and Wind Ridge. It's both easy to find and a surprise when stumbled upon. It's like a thousand other Douglas firs that dot the sunny southeastern side of this deep mountain vale, and singular in every way.

It is a prayer tree. Around its roots are a circle of stones with an entrance that allows access to the tree's circumference. Approach the tree as I often do from the path that winds by its bottom, and soon all manner of offerings appear: beads and glass baubles scattered in the dust among its roots; handwritten notes, an empty vial of homeopathic medicine, coins and a key wedged in its thick bark; notes and pouches suspended from its branches by string. A spiral of twigs is laid out in a neat pattern on the bare earth below the spreading limbs.

I found this tree by accident on one of my first runs through the woods above my home, more than a year ago. I've had other such companions throughout my days on the trail over this lifetime. In high school, I named a spreading American beech "Phaedrus" after a character in

Zen and the Art of Motorcycle Maintenance, and mourned its loss when my precious woods were cut to make way for the 427 toll highway. When I lived in Harvie Heights, near Canmore, for six years in the 1990s, I named a massive Engelmann spruce "Issrigill," one of the pillars of the earth in Roman mythology.

By the time I worked at Royal Roads University, I had stopped naming my favourite trees, but found them nevertheless. On a campus full of extraordinary trees there was a massive Norway maple that at its base was six feet across. I found a way to run by that tree almost every day I was on campus, and it never failed to fill me with a sense of magical wonder.

But never have I come across a tree that is so obviously important to so many other people. Despite the conspicuous adoration felt for this particular tree, I've yet to meet anybody there on my dozens of runs past it. And that's just as well, because for me the sort of druidic reverence I and others evidently feel for this tree is best practised in private.

On my circuitous routes through the woods and meadows along the slopes of Grotto Mountain, I often let whimsy decide my course, so I'm always pleasantly surprised to find myself at the base of this tree. So it was the other day. I stopped running and walked through the opening in the stones. For some reason I have it in my head that the people leaving offerings here are young. I figure most adults have lost the sense of wonder and suspended judgment required to leave a prayer in the form of a note, a coin or a key in such a place. I wanted to offer something but didn't have anything to leave: somehow I didn't think the wrapper from a Clif Shot could be interpreted as anything but garbage.

But I did have something I needed to take with me. I circled the tree a few times, trying to quiet my racing mind. There has been a lot of pain in the world of late; a lot of pain in my family too. Several dear family members are sick. Two of the people I love the most in this world are facing the end of the journey. I do not want them to leave just yet. A friend is passing through dark times, suffering from a deep depression. And on the same day I was saying my prayers at this tree, the father of friends I grew up with – a man whose presence when I was a child seemed like it would last forever – was being put to rest after a massive heart attack.

There were other prayers to offer. Last week a child was born to friends who are love incarnate, and this little boy will grow up deeply cared for and cherished. They named him Isaiah and recalled the words: "Though the mountains be shaken and the hills be removed, yet my unfailing love for you will not be shaken nor my covenant of peace be removed." (Isaiah 54:10)

When we need something that we believe is beyond our control, we sometimes pray for it.

More money. More health. More choices. More time.

I do not believe there is a supernatural being to pray to,

and nobody will respond to my supplication except the wind and the sun. So why do I find myself praying when I run past this tree?

Because when I am at my best I know that all life is a prayer. Because every moment, every word, every breath is a prayer. Prayer focuses our intent, and calls together the sometimes magical and often mundane coagulation of hope and belief and the power of our thoughts to create reality.

And because sometimes prayer is all we have. And sometimes prayer is all we need.

And so, at the base of the tree where others have left gifts, I leave love and courage for my family and friends who are struggling to hold on to life, and offer the gift of hope and peace for baby Isaiah. And then, the afternoon sun warming my face and the wind speeding my steps, I keep running through the prayer-filled woods.

BEDTIME STORIES

One: there is no end

The boys and I read a lot of books at bedtime. Both Rio and Silas are voracious readers; Rio is into Rick Riordan's various mythology thrillers, while Silas will read just about anything Dr. Seuss has ever penned. A little while ago we read *The Old Man and the Sea* together. For a while we were making our way through *Watership Down*, and more recently we read Richard Bach's *There's No Such Place as Far Away*.

Bach, as you might recall, penned *Jonathan Livingston Seagull*, which didn't do much for me, and *Illusions*, which did. *No Such Place as Far Away* is about a series of birds in conversation with Rae, an osprey who is on his way to celebrate his birthday at a party. Along the way he receives as gifts a series of oblique life lessons from his friends. From the seagull, Rae learns that "not being known doesn't stop the truth from being true," and from the hummingbird, he learns to ask the question: "Can miles truly separate us from friends? If you want to be [together], aren't you already there?"

All good lessons, but a little obscure. The last lesson, however, was a whopper:

> You have no birthday because you have always

lived; you were never born, and never will you die. You are not the child of the people you call mother and father, but their fellow-adventurer on a bright journey to understand the things that are.

"What do you think that means?" I asked Silas and Rio as we snuggled together.

Neither boy was certain. It dawned on me what Bach was saying: "There is no beginning and no end; not as we have come to believe in them. Life isn't a linear progression from birth through adulthood to death," I say, knowing that I'm treading on thin ice. Talk of death is difficult, especially before bed. "What makes you who you are, and what makes me who I am" – I pinch Silas's cheeks, not to illustrate the point, but just because they are so pinchable – "has always been here. We're just constantly being rearranged."

I'm not sure if that made any sense. I still don't.

Two: *presence is your present*

Sometimes one boy or the other has a hard time falling asleep. Not often, but from time to time. One of the things I've been teaching my children is the gift of the present moment.

If Rio or Silas is frustrated because they can't sleep, I remind them of "present moment awareness." This is one of the most important lessons we can learn; this moment is all the life we will ever know. Both the past and future are illusion. This moment is the only moment we can live in.

How does this help a seven- or a ten-year-old fall asleep? I remind them that in this moment they are safe and have nothing to fear. I remind them that in this moment they are secure in their beds, comfortable and so deeply loved. Safe in that knowledge, not worrying about tomorrow or contemplating yesterday, they can stay grounded in present moment awareness. I sometimes suggest they focus on their breath, as I try so desperately to do while meditating.

Recently we've been reciting that mantra plucked from *Peaceful Warrior*:

What time is it?

Now.

Where are you?

Here.

What are you?

This moment.

So I guess it should have come as no surprise when, after a recent story-reading and cuddle with Silas, he reminded me of the importance of the present. As I sometimes do, I told him: "I can't wait to see you in the morning."

He smirked and in a wry tone said, "Stephie, present moment awareness!"

Three: the purpose of life

From time to time all the bedtime stories and the reminders about the present moment don't help, and one boy or the other can't fall asleep.

Such was the case a few nights ago. Silas was sad, missing his other household, and sore with growing pains. For several hours Jenn and I calmed him down and held him and he would drift off to sleep, only to wake again. Finally we went to bed ourselves, and a little while later I heard chatter from the boys' bedroom, but it stopped, so I fell back to sleep.

When I got up to write the next morning, around 5:30, Silas was asleep on the floor. His comforter, not used during the warm summer months, had been bunched up to make a bed there. He was fast asleep.

Later, when Rio got up, he told me the rest of the story. Hoping to be able to fall asleep himself, and unable to because Silas was sad, he had climbed down from the top bunk and made a nest on the floor for his little brother, using extra pillows and the comforter to create a cocoon. Then the two of them had curled up there and fallen asleep together. Sometime in the early morning hours, Rio had gone back to his own bed.

It's the best bedtime story of all; it's the story of our purpose: to love one another.

We are having a wonderful love affair together.

AUTUMN TRAILS

I went for a run yesterday for the first time in six months. I hadn't run since April. It's the second time I've taken such a hiatus in the last eighteen months, and I was beginning to worry that maybe my days of trail running were coming to a close. But yesterday it was a perfect bluebird day; the aspens that cloak the hillsides above my Canmore home were ablaze in yellows and gold, and I've been itching to feel the steady rhythm of motion I've come to love.

My knees have been in rough shape of late. In April I woke one morning limping, and it persisted for weeks. I took a break. I finished the ski season and then rode my mountain bike three or four times a week and learned to see the world at a very different speed. It was a lot of fun, and I got in decent shape, and my knees didn't hurt as much.

But yesterday the sun and the colours made me throw caution to the wind. I took it slowly, worried that my knees might protest, or my lungs give out, or my legs turn to stone. But none of this happened. I glided up the trail as if I hadn't taken six months off, and after an hour-and-a-half of running on the dazzling aspen benchlands, I felt very good indeed. I didn't care if it was my first run or my last; I wasn't running for anything but the sheer joy of being in motion on a stunningly beautiful day. I felt once again the feeling of inseparability between myself and the landscape – between myself and everything else in the universe – and didn't worry if it would ever happen again. It was enough to be alive, in motion and perfect stillness all at once.

I thought about the months when I hadn't been running as a prolonged period of stillness, even though I'd been riding my bike and walking nearly every day.

Inside of motion there is stillness, and in stillness, motion. The ancient symbol of Taoism is the Tai Chi: the black and white swirl with a dot of black in the white and a dot of white in the black. These two halves are not opposites coming together, but parts of the same whole, working in harmony.

There is a still point in motion that occurs when the runner, the rider, the walker, moves in a way that is completely free of effort, and in a manner where the barrier between ourselves and nature evaporates. At this moment we touch the perfection of creation and open a door to the mysterious fabric of the universe to reveal itself in us.

Just so, in stillness – meditation – there is motion. The circle of breathing that creates a rhythm also opens the door to a glimpse into the infinite between our cluttered thoughts.

Motion and stillness, working in harmony, can be a portal through which we glimpse the true nature of the universe, and our beautiful place within it.

The sun was setting as I wove my way home, the bright woods breezing past. I felt the familiar cadence of breath, the steady beat of my feet on the leaf-strewn path, the rhythmic pulse of heart and blood and bone as I trotted down familiar trails.

Don't be afraid to stop, I told myself, and don't be afraid to start again. That's all this is, a simple rebirth. Every single day.

TRAIL NOTES: PART FIVE

Where is home for you?

What act of graceful surrender might
make you feel more at peace?

What is weighing you down?
What can you let go of to lighten up?

What can you do today to help you
connect with your purpose in life?

Imagine that you left anger and fear behind you forever.

What will you do today that will bring you peace?

Start Again

We come to the end of the trail, but the journey is not over. There is no beginning and no end; just a series of revolutions around the sun, through the stars, and back again to where we began. But we are different, you and I. We have grown together, and have circled upward toward heaven, toward nirvana.

We have found stillness and then kept on running.

The shell breaks and the suffering seems to come to an end, and there is peace. There is always another layer of shell through which we must push, but helping hands and a loving heart make the pain bearable. And we know this path; we have run this way many times before. We shall run this way again. And we are not alone.

Gratitude

I wish to express my deepest gratitude to my wife, Jenn Hoffman, for being my teacher and partner on this journey through life. This was not an easy book to write, and I am grateful to her for allowing me to lay bare so much of our lives in these pages. You are the love of my life.

My gratitude also to J, my best friend, who throughout the time encapsulated in these pages was a constant source of strength and support. He still is.

Thanks also to Dan Spinner, who asked all the hard questions, and James Pratt, who always listened. Thank you to Kat Wiebe, who forgave me, and encouraged me to forgive myself, and stayed my friend and supported me with a generous heart. Thanks also to her husband, and my friend, Andy Arts for his role in my life and that of our children, and for being a part of this tale.

A special thank-you to Sarah Pullman, Bruce Elkin, Jessica Kluthe, Jason Meyers, Hal Dundas and George Evashuk, who read the manuscript for this book and provided the necessary tough love to help make it a better story.

My deep gratitude to Don Gorman and the staff at

RMB | Rocky Mountain Books, who have taken a risk by publishing a very non-traditional book about running. My sincere thanks to Peter Norman for being a gentle, yet firm, copy-editor.

And my love and thanks go to Rio and Silas, just learning that they have so much more to teach their father than he has to teach them. May you, my sons, find peace and an end to suffering in your lifetime.

ABOUT THE AUTHOR

Stephen Legault is a writer, photographer, full-time conservation activist and organizational development consultant who lives in Canmore, Alberta, with his wife, Jenn, and two children, Rio and Silas. He is the author of seven other books, including *Carry Tiger to Mountain: The Tao of Activism and Leadership* and the TouchWood Editions mystery novels *The Vanishing Track*, *The Slickrock Paradox* and *The Third Riel Conspiracy*.